BOUNDLESS: 2023

THE ANTHOLOGY OF THE
RIO GRANDE VALLEY
INTERNATIONAL POETRY FESTIVAL

FLOWERSONG
PRESS

FlowerSong Press
McAllen, Texas 78501
Copyright © 2023 FlowerSong Press

ISBN: 978-1-953447-28-9

Published by FlowerSong Press
in the United States of America.
www.flowersongpress.com

Set in Adobe Garamond Pro

Typeset by Priscilla Celina Suarez
Cover Image and Design by Edward Vidaurre

NOTICE: SCHOOLS AND BUSINESSES
FlowerSong Press offers copies of this book at quantity discount with bulk
purchase for educational, business, or sales promotional use. For information,
please email the Publisher at info@flowersongpress.com.

BOUNDLESS: 2023

THE ANTHOLOGY OF THE
RIO GRANDE VALLEY
INTERNATIONAL POETRY FESTIVAL

FLOWERSONG
PRESS

Selected & Edited by

Linda Romero
Eduardo Villarreal de los Reyes
& Edward Vidaurre

V.I.P.F.

Rio Grande Valley
International Poetry Festival

Boundless is the official anthology of the Rio Grande Valley
International Poetry Festival (VIPF), founded in 2008 by Daniel
García Ordaz and Brenda Nettles Riojas. VIPF is held annually
the last weekend in April in deep South Texas as a celebration of
National Poetry Month. Directed by Edward Vidaurre.

www.valleypoetryfest.org

Table of Contents

Introduction xvii
  by Linda Romero

Introducción xix
  by Linda Romero

In honor of xxi

translingualism as a praxis: an essay xxiii
  by jo reyes-boitel

I | SELECTED POEMS BY LINDA ROMERO & EDUARDO VILLAREAL DE LOS REYES

Letter to Márquez on the Anniversary of His Winning an Award ......
  by Marcella Prokop

In And Of 4
  by Bruce McRae

Si usted quisiera 5
   by Adriana Rodríguez

Broken 6
   by Aleksandra Lekić Vujisić

El libro es como un mar 7
   by Alekhine Rebaza

Out The Window 8
   by Peace Nkeiruka Maduako

La noche eterna 9
   by Andrés Mijangos Labastida

I Stand With You 10
   by Doug Croft

Me deben tiempo 11
   by Rubén Gerardo Santos Lezcano

The Butterfly Lovers 12
Also the tragic love story of 梁山伯 *and* 祝英臺
   by Chim Sher Ting

Cuando la voz duerme y el corazón habla 13
   by Tania Jasso Blancas

MERGE 14
   by Dee Allen

Andares 15
   by Nelson Roque Pereira

Whispers from the womb 16
   by Abubakar Auwal

Renacer del Ave Fénix 17
   por Bertha Galán

The Probable Absurdity of Our Existence 18
  by Christopher T. Dabrowski

Luces de neón 19
  por Yonnier Torres Rodríguez

Unfold My Heart 20
  by Tabassum Tahmina Shagufta Hussein

Mi gesto 21
  por Santiago Domínguez

THIS INEXPLICABLE NEED 22
  by Edward Lee

EL GRITO 23
  por Rodrigo Miguel Quintero

Insensitivity, 'The Fall' and Zen Monasteries 24
  by Douglas Colston

Identidad Desconocida 25
  por Miriam Romero

Florecer 26
  por Estrella Gracia González

KILCOLMAN 27
  by Anita Howard

EL ERRANTE 28
  por Rolando Reyes López

Youngblood en la Frontera 29
  by William David

La constelación de los dos amantes 30
  por Gabriel González Núñez

Inside out I see 31
 by Olivier Pascalin

Migrante 32
 por Chepy Salinas Domínguez

Love Like Tacos 33
 by Juan Manuel Perez

Una plegaria más 34
 por José Luis Moreno

My Chest was Like the Coconut 36
 by Stephen Douglas Wright

A veces quiero dejar de escribir 38
 por Roswel Borges Castellanos

Cafuné 39
 by Nancy Jo Allen

FINAL Y PRINCIPIO 40
 por Wendy B. Lara

Provenance Of My Rage 41
 by Megha Sood

Migajas de paraíso 42
 por Felix Cardoso

RETURN TO THE VALLEY 43
 by Margaret Cantu-Sanchez

Baijiu/ Wong Fei vuelve a casa 45
 por José Rodolfo Espinosa Silva

DESIRE 46
 by Aldo Cristian Méndez Castillo

Escape......47
 por Irlyan del Carmen Hernández Sosa de Bacalar

MULTI-STOREYED 48
 by Sharanya B

Astrología 49
 por Ana Saldaña

Gone Shopping 50
 by Allan Lake

no te nombro 51
 por Alejandro Zapata Espinosa

The Poor Man 52
 by Binod Dawadi

Como el viento 53
 por Ramiro Hernández Restrepo

Something Long Gone 54
 by Candace Meredith

CUANDO NO ME MIRAS 55
 por Víctor Hugo Orduña Silguero

Sundays 57
 by E. Martin Pedersen

Adagio sognante 58
 por Eduardo Omar Honey Escandón

Non places 59
 by Jackie Kabir

Lenguaje milenario 60
 por Alejandro Chang Hernández

This is not a poem 61
  by Roxana Arroyo

FELIS POETRIS CATUS 62
  por G. Libedinsky

MIS OJOS HECHIZAN 64
  por Claudia Elisa Saquicela Novillo

The Line Between 65
  by Thomas Ray Garcia

ashé andino 66
  por Enrique Manuel Infante Ángeles

Aurora Borealis Teach Me To Utter I Love You 67
  by Kim Malinowski

LO QUE FUI, LO QUE SOY 68
  por Baltazar Cordero Tamez

Behold The Raging River 69
  by Dorthy LaVern Spencer McCarthy

Changüí 70
  por Iván Medina

Luz de estrellas 71
  por Antonio Ramírez Córdova

Union Pacific Northwest 72
  by Mike Owsley

Pajarito 73
  por Walter Alexis Velásquez Mendoza

Shelf Life 74
  by Mark Fleisher

The Ancients 75
   by Carmen Gray

The Cost 76
   by Terry Allen

Searching 77
   by Trev Wainwright

Walls......78
   by Carmen Calatayud

Atonement Three 79
   by John Chinaka Onyeche

Husband is Putting on Blues Records 80
   by Adrian Ernesto Cepeda

We Used to Live on Icebergs 81
   by Gerry Rodriguez

We Do not Want your Privilege 82
   by Rolando Serna

That Photo on the Wall 84
   by Gerald Jatzek

3.25.2022 85
   by Julia-Paz

To Draw Water From A Barren Well 86
   by Ashlynn Delias

Ars Poetica 87
   by Elisa A. Garza

MASKS 88
   by Luisa Govela

IT COULD HAPPEN AGAIN *89*
by Sandra Dolores Gómez Amador

ghosts 90
by Michael Gerleman

Antonio Orendain, ¡Presente! 91
by Nephtalí De León

Sometimes 93
by Enedina Irene

BESIDE BROKEN CLOUDS 95
by Uchechukwu Onyedikam

The Gathering of Faithfuls 96
by Mohammed U. Yusuf

Vaults of autumn 97
by Joselin Mejía Garcia, Mexico

The Boxer 98
by G.G. (Giana Gallardo) Hesterberg

In Ixtli In Yolotl: Hay Cosas que Nunca se te Darán de Vuelta 100
by Joann González

Esperanza Is Another Name for Hope 101
by Jean Hackett

I Majored in Writing and Now I am a Copywriter 102
by Paula Andrea Córdova García

Drop of Time 103
by Michael Owens

Dine in 104
by Spartakos Anagnostaras

Jenny in the Bottle 105
  by Laura Peña

Driving Next to the Llano River in Marble Falls, Texas 106
  by Shannon Hardwick

Walk With My Dead Tía Abuela At the Neighborhood Festival 107
  by Violeta Garza

Aftermath 108
  by John C. Mannone

The burden tossed between tousled sheets 109
  by Victoria Lopez

Nuestra Vida 110
  by Vito del Valle

My Lovely Valley 111
  by Yelitza Tibisai Saenz

Mi Valle Querida 112
  by Yelitza Tibisai Saenz

DIVIDED 113
  by Érika Elisa Garza

An Egyptian folk tale 114
  by Shaswata Gangopadhyay

Building Blocks 115
  by Alan Cherian Puthenpurayil

I Tried to Give You my Star 116
  by Gustavo Barahona-López

Phoenix 117
  by Jasmin Garcia

I always knew you were a portrait 118
by Mark Esperanza

Magic 120
by Gabriella Gutiérrez y Muhs

THE BAMBOO GROVE BENT DOWN 121
by Guna Moran

A Letter to my Baby's Twin Myoma 122
by Denise Melanie Du Lagrosa

Lodestar 123
by PW Covington

Bendición 124
by Yari "Porta Rock"

Who's That Girl? 126
by Diosa Xochiquetzalcóatl

Hoy llevo el altar en mi boca 128
por Diosa Xochiquetzalcóatl

love/death 129
by Karen Cline-Tardiff

Prayer for Milk Weed 130
by Karen Cline-Tardiff

Los sauces 132
por J. Villarreal

The Willows 133
por J. Villarreal

II | FROM OUR EDITORS

In All the Days Like Today 137
  by Linda Romero

I Never Knew Grief Until You Were Gone 138
  by Linda Romero

Hay días 139
  por Eduardo Villarreal de los Reyes

Péndulo 140
  por Eduardo Villarreal de los Reyes

Gravedad 141
  por Eduardo Villarreal de los Reyes

River 142
  by Edward Vidaurre

I HAVEN'T BEEN TO CHURCH 143
  by Edward Vidaurre

III. | FROM OUR YOUTH

Sola 147
  por Yadira Mejía

Viviendo en soledad 148
  por Alef Hernández

Life in a shell/La vida en un caparazón 149
  by Juan Elizondo

Una amiga 150
  por Brisa Adame-Peña

Poema 1 151
   por Susana Leal

Qué pasará 152
   por Dulce Mata

Cuando muramos 153
   por América Quintero

La mejor estudiante 154
   por Anayeli

Azul/Alguna persona/Mía 155
   por Crystalynn Chávez

Nuestra Navidad 156
   por Leonardo R.

Indecisa/Este día/Contigo 157
   por Sarah Garza

Poema 1 158
   por Ángela Colón

El árbol leal/The loyal tree 159
   por Diego Treviño

i am 161
   by Luisa Vidaurre

IV. | VIPF CONTRIBUTORS/ COLABORADORES
     DE VIPF 165

V | EDITORS BIOS 187

Introduction

by Linda Romero

Several years ago I went to the Border Wall for a poetry reading. I noticed patches of sunflowers growing wild. They grew in front of and behind the wall, and even out from under it. In their wildness, those sunflowers would grow in the midst of whatever they faced and in whatever environment they found themselves rooted to, parched by our Valley drought or not. Their growth and determination seemed boundless. And just as sunflowers have no boundaries, neither does poetry.

Whether we write for ourselves or to share with others in readings or by submitting to publications, what prompts somebody to put pen to paper and document what stirs the human spirit is an act of bravery in and of itself. When someone tells me they're afraid to write because of what others would think or ask what purpose it has: I always tell them their words had purpose the moment they were written because those words served them, the writer. Just the act of writing serves us. And if no one else sees that writing, so be it. But how much more power do those words carry when someone across the world can read those words and be affected the same way? In a way the reader feels they are not alone when emotions seem without words. That's the power of poetry. That's what the poems in this year's *Boundless* anthology do.

Poetry submitted to us in the Rio Grande Valley of South Texas from the reaches of Nigeria, the Philippines, Mexico, Italy, Bangladesh, France, Ireland, England, Greece, and the list goes on … as well as local submissions from the Rio Grande Valley and around the United States and Canada were such a joy for me to read and experience and grow from as a poet. What I love more is that *Boundless* and the Rio Grande Valley International Poetry Festival make available a space for poets of varying experience to submit and be welcomed for the shared love of poetry, and bring us all together, whether in person or virtually.

Rest assured that every submission I read, accepted or not, I read aloud. I spoke all the words of every poem I read into the universe, even perhaps more than once. Not just in acknowledgement of the piece of writing; but of the bravery in each submission. I read aloud in an effort to further resonate with their ideas, the texture of their words, and the emotions they brought to me.

I am thankful for the opportunity to have served as editor for this year's anthology. And I thank all the poets for contributing to the human experience through their words.

In gratitude,

Linda Feliciana Romero
Editor

Introducción

por Linda Romero

Hace varios años fui al Muro Fronterizo para una lectura de poesía. Noté parches de girasoles creciendo silvestres. Crecieron delante y detrás de la pared, e incluso fuera de ella. En su naturaleza salvaje, esos girasoles crecerían en medio de lo que enfrentarán y en cualquier entorno al que se encontraban arraigados, resecos por la sequía de nuestro Valle o no. Su crecimiento y determinación parecían ilimitados. Y así como los girasoles no tienen límites, tampoco la poesía.

Ya sea que escribamos para nosotros mismos o para compartir con otros en lecturas o enviando publicaciones, lo que impulsa a alguien a poner la pluma en el papel y documentar lo que agita el espíritu humano es un acto de valentía en sí mismo. Cuando alguien me dice que tiene miedo de escribir por lo que otros pensarían o preguntaría qué propósito tiene: Siempre les digo que sus palabras tenían un propósito en el momento en que fueron escritas porque esas palabras les sirvieron a ellos, el escritor. Sólo el acto de escribir nos sirve. Y si nadie más ve esa escritura, que así sea. Pero, ¿cuánto más poder tienen esas palabras cuando alguien en todo el mundo puede leer esas palabras y verse afectado de la misma manera? En cierto modo, el lector siente que no está solo cuando las emociones parecen sin palabras. Ese es el poder de la poesía. Eso es lo que hacen los poemas de la antología Boundless de este año.

Poesía enviada a nosotros en el Valle del Río Grande del sur de Texas desde los confines de Nigeria, Filipinas, México, Italia, Bangladesh, Francia, Irlanda, Inglaterra, Grecia, y la lista continúa ... así como las presentaciones locales del Valle del Río Grande y alrededor de los Estados Unidos y Canadá fueron una gran alegría para mí leer, experimentar y crecer como poeta. Lo que más me gusta es que Boundless y el Festival Internacional de Poesía del Valle del Río Grande ponen a disposición un espacio para que poetas de diversa experiencia se presenten y sean bienvenidos por el amor compartido por la poesía, y nos unan a todos, ya sea en persona o virtualmente.

Tenga la seguridad de que cada envío que leo, aceptado o no, lo leo en voz alta. Dije todas las palabras de cada poema que leí en el universo, incluso quizás más de una vez. No solo en reconocimiento de la pieza de escritura; sino de la valentía en cada presentación. Leí en voz alta en un esfuerzo por resonar aún más con sus ideas, la textura de sus palabras y las emociones que me trajeron.

Estoy agradecida por la oportunidad de haber servido como editora de la antología de este año con mis amigos en poesía Edward Vidaurre y Eduardo Villarreal De Los Reyes y agradezco a todos los poetas por contribuir a la experiencia humana a través de sus palabras.

En agradecimiento,

Linda Feliciana Romero
Editora

Dedication

IN HONOR OF:

Jan Seale. 2012 Texas State Poet Laureate, McAllen, Texas
Emmy Pérez, 2020 Texas Poet Laureate, McAllen, Texas
Daniel Garcia Ordaz, 2023 City of McAllen Poet Laureate

IN MEMORIAM:

Dr. Gloria Evangelina Anzaldúa
Jovita González
Dr. Américo Paredes
Raúl R. Salinas
Trinidad Sánchez
Benito Pastoriza Iyodo
Eugene "Gene" Navogrodsky
Wendy Barker
Michael Rothenberg

todx vuelven:
translingualism as a praxis.

by jo reyes-boitel

I learned the word semaphore today. I am one of those who grew up in under-funded schools where I had to grab at whatever book I could because I wanted to read. I still have words floating around my head that I don't always know how to use or how to pronounce. Still, I realized I knew a version of this word in another way. Semaphores are flags, signals, across great distances, like the flag folks who direct planes on the tarmac. Or the way I can share eyes with a friend when one first enters a cafe where the other has been waiting. Flags will show apology, excitement, and question all in one wave. Held momentarily on the face of the person across from you. Like a secret between just you two. It asks you to be aware.

I've been thinking about seahorses, the way the males parent their as yet unhatched babies, while the women skirt across waters having completed their job. I wasn't thinking of this part of their life in particular. I just remembered this. But that reminded me of the graphic making its way through social media of a black horse walking. It's a gif. A moveable picture. The frame of the image asked if we saw it walking forward or backward as backward meant we were right brained and the expectation that we are more creative is offered to us like a gift. As though we've run through horses to fight for our art, caught under foot, dust plumes in our face, coloring our clothing. Well, I realize now I've bought into the idea, even if I didn't remember what they were selling. Our ideas and our identity is created piecemeal.

There's a horse in the brain. Well, a sea horse, or from the proto-German *harss*, a horse-like monster shaped like the hook and *s* of a seahorse, with its skeletal rigidity too, sitting as our hippocampus, which rules our drive for embodied knowledge through a cocktail of memory, emotion, and the nervous system. These three work together to consolidate memory into something we can access and continually return to.[1] The etymology of the word hippocampus is *hippo* from the Latin horse and *kampus* meaning sea monster. I'm still thinking of language too, at least passively, which my multilingual brain tries to find connections for. I didn't mean to move away from the word semaphore but it instantly reminds me of Ruben Blades' song "En El Semaforo", at the intersection of two streets[2]. A streetlight. A momentary idea. A scene unfolding before our eyes. Blades is older now, with a ton of records under his belt and even a presidential run, but I still think of Blades on the rooftop in the movie *Crossover Dreams*,[3] where, after all the success of a salsa career has disappeared, he returns to the sound of the city and his two espresso-tinted clave sticks hitting 1-2 / 1-2-3. Rhythm is the root of language. It carries meaning. It's no surprise sounds like mmm sooth. Mama, mamey, mambo, mano, milk, mouth. Words that let you sink in like a warm tub. Language is a sea monster, floating through our bodies, intimate but often unknowable. But it wants us to know ourselves. As much as we can in a world where memory is herencia but inheritance isn't guaranteed. As Rubén Blades sings: "bajo el árbol del pasado / cuantas veces nos ponemos a sonar / todos vuelven por la ruta del recuerdo…"

Translingualism is a phenomenon newly named but that has always been a part of our language, our cultural expression, and our attempt at self and wholeness – from the first moment we attributed meaning to the sounds rising in our mouths. *Trans-* meaning across and *lingual* meaning having to do with languages/tongues. Across tongues feels like something Gloria Anzaldúa would say, situating it in nepantla. Translingualism was something she did easily both in her seminal work *Borderlands/La Frontera: The New Mestiza* and in person, switching from friendly – nearly flirty – to scholarly, to necessary. Here I claim that even if using one recognizable language the way we express ourselves is a translingual expression because we speak in multiplicities. Who we are is tethered to all of what has been passed down, what we have experienced, and what we have managed to cultivate. Think of the sea horse, how they tether themselves to coral or each other to stay in communication. The root of us is language but that language is ever expanding. If you doubt this consider the many ways a parent calls out your name and how, instinctively, there's an understanding of their mood, what

---

[1] https://uselessetymology.com/2017/11/24/the-etymology-of-hippocampus/
[2] https://www.youtube.com/watch?v=5CxGIwkDNgc
[3] https://www.youtube.com/watch?v=9exubo1xDZE

they may need, and the reminder of what childhood guilt you might be carrying. Or, the good friend who you don't call by name but by diosa, hermosa, querida, cabrona. Or, the raised eyebrow of a drag performer when you hand them a $5 bill because they sang "El Chico del Apartamento 512" while dressed up as Selena and you realize how much your heart needed this. Like food. Like touch.

And still sometimes we are that horse, running over everything in our wake, smashing it until every recognizable piece becomes a sandy powder clinging like glitter. This makes me think of sentence diagrams, where a simple phrase carries multiple meanings. Flags, if you will, directing us to multiple endings. Take this line from a mini-poetic essay I wrote a while back:

> She took a role she never wanted and somehow, she thought she was expected to hold the weight of that decision until the lilt of freedom was truly gone.[45]

It's about my mother. And my voice here is passive, quietly threaded into this line because my "narrator" voice is empathetic to the powerless but angry moment my mother is in. This voice raises awareness but it also distances, pushed further by the rolling feel of the opening words' iambic pentameter. The "she" repeated again and again indicates the incredible role this person has to the narrator but also the weight of what she carries. The word "lilt" here one of the few stressed syllables that also carries a lightness, only to be defused by the double unstressed ending. And the sentence itself is so long! It is almost impossible to be completed within one breath. Thankfully there's a comma but the desperation for another breath appears just before "lilt", making the possibility for freedom an impossibility. And don't forget that silence is also a language we hold. Like the person, arms flailing, who flags to the largeness before them despite the incredible effort needed to corral it all. I could have stayed in the positive and loving images of this essay but the only way we really rejoice is to acknowledge all that this world offers us, whether beneficial or heartbreaking.

Translingualism gives us freedom to say hard things. To combine the multiple languages we carry (tones, registers, English, Spanish, creole, French, Celia Cruz' *Azucar!* declarations, ALL the ways through) in a language that lives in our bodies. Language that arrives as music and is delivered through a poetry

[4] https://www.etymonline.com/search?q=hippocampus

[5] From https://www.latinxproject.nyu.edu/intervenxions/writing-the-mother-wound-a-mothers-day-anthology

uniquely ours. It is an act of decolonization if we want to get academic – and indeed transligualism is now studied and pedagogy has been developed that incorporates it – but isn't decoloniality, for writers, another way of saying *here is what roots me* and *here is what I rejoice in* and *here is what I have experienced that has changed me but has not killed me*. Tethered but buoyant. Finding the clave sitting in our bodies, that 1-2 / 1-2-3 that wakes up our mind to the world around us.

I.

Poems Selected by
Linda Romero &
Eduardo Villarreal de los Reyes

Poemas seleccionados por
Linda Romero &
Eduardo Villarreal de los Reyes

Letter to Márquez on the Anniversary of His Winning an Award
by Marcella Prokop

Has it been 154 years already? Or just 40?
Perhaps we have passed only 120 days
since our last correspondence,
your words, direct to me from the past
and the present,
have forewarned of this future
from some time and place you did not yet know.
Each image translucent and tangible as a wing,
every line flutters on parchment yellowed
like fallen flowers.
Dearest friend,
I still do not understand if it is destiny
or determination that drives this body
like a pendulum,
these thousand whirring clocks,
my cells, ticking away each moment.
Is my nostalgia for this place,
or that time, more dream than memory?
This morning, a rooster crows,
his greatness lingering in echo.
When again I read your words,
will they then reveal the answers?

In And Of
by Bruce McRae

A painting of the world
as it is at the moment.
Including turtles and tax returns.
Including carnations and palo verde.
With candlewax and dog-bark and cod roe,
the myopic painter mixing metaphors.
He stirs colours.

In this painting are a pig's knuckles
and thigh bone of a Chaldean general.
There's a coin dropped down a grate,
neither head nor tails.
A child is bawling for its mother.
There's a car crash on the autobahn,
for which death is certain.
A deft hand has shaped a horse's mane
and braid of wheat-coloured grasses.
It's captured light's moody temperament,
sunsets of pinks and purple strands.
A contented cow. A miserable coxswain.

Millions of years in the making, this painting
contains pocket lint and buttons of ivory.
And there are you and I, we're walking by the mill,
the artist having it rain. Impeccably portrayed,
we seem oblivious to time and love.
Stood defiant to death's erasure.

Si usted quisiera
by Adriana Rodríguez

¿Será posible que usted
pueda acompañarme
en esta tarde nublada sin la luz
de su magnánime presencia?

¿Será posible que usted
cielo de mis mañanas
se escape de su divinidad
y venga a calmar mis delirios?

¿Será posible que usted
amor de todas mis vidas
baje de su enaltecida gloria
a posar sus labios a mis horas?

¿Será posible que usted
beba conmigo todos mis vinos
y nos embriaguemos de miradas
hasta que amanezca?

¿Será posible que usted
me regale sus manos, sus ojos
sus abrazos, sus besos, su amor
en esta mi solitaria existencia?

Digo ¿No sé? ¡Sí usted quisiera!

Broken
by Aleksandra Lekić Vujisić

It feels like waking up next to a ghost
and craving for life
and getting lost,
and I want to hold the girl that
I used to be,
tell her that ancient secret for me
doesn't mean more than a sweet lie –
come on little girl,
be brave, don't cry.

Broken, like a glass of wine
after a fight,
broken with all that was mine,
without no light,
broken like a preacher of forgotten prayers,
like a painting with no colours and layers,
and never asking the reason why –
come on little girl,
be brave, don't cry.

You have left me so many times before
but I always tend to ask for more,
I never stop and never believe –
come on little girl,
be brave, just leave.

El libro es como un mar
by Alekhine Rebaza

El libro es como un mar,
me baño en sus aguas
y pasan las páginas
como pasan las olas,
cóncavas, frescas y rotundas (poderosas).
El olor del libro
es tan agradable como la brisa del mar,
el masaje del líquido es la letra,
la corriente, sus palabras que me llevan.
Hacia el atardecer,
habré acabado el libro del mar
y disfrutaré lo que me ha dejado,
tal vez la visión más bella: la puesta de sol.
La historia del libro ya es parte de mí,
como el mar y las olas.

Out The Window
by Peace Nkeiruka Maduako

I had a dream
Where by the window I stood
On a cool spring noon
And there from the woods
You were coming back to me.
I had a dream
That one day someday
You will come back to me,
And into your eyes I'll stare
While we dance someplace,
In a field pure green
Under a clear blue sky.

I had a dream
That I looked out the window
And saw you afar
And my poor heart leaped
At the sight of your smile.
So I get up early
And stand a little
Looking out the window,
For maybe I'd see you,
Maybe you'd come back to me.

La noche eterna
by Andrés Mijangos Labastida

llega sin que nos demos cuenta
dentro de nosotros
crece en esos recovecos del alma
que nadie observa

La noche eterna llega un día
                                en que al abrir los párpados
nos sentimos radiantes

Llega y nuestro cuerpo
se siente aliviado
ir hasta el fondo
también es liberarse

I Stand With You
by Doug Croft

I stand with you sister
I stand with you brother
No matter the skin tone
No matter the color

I stand with you
Against racial discrimination
I stand with you
In social unification

I'll stand with you
Opposing violence and disparity
I stand with you
In peaceful solidarity

This saying keeps me reminded
It's not separation of me or you
It's about all together
Them, is us too

I stand with you
For there is no inferiority
I am with you
Standing out of silent majority

Until those of privilege
Stand with those denied
America cannot be great
United or unified

I stand with you
In this land of brave and free
I stand with you
You and you and you and me

Me deben tiempo
by Rubén Gerardo Santos Lezcano

Soy hombre a quien le deben tiempo
porque alguna vez cedió las horas,
ese contar pausado de mil momentos
que hoy, casi dolido, por fuerza añora.

Cedí mi tiempo a más de un anhelo
que como desnuda mujer mostraban
la azarosa ardentía y el sol sin velo
que, sobre el reto, sobrio me ataban.

Mi tiempo lo entregué sin reticencias
al conjuro del pan siempre sufrido,
al clarín estimulante y a la paciencia
de buscar los oropeles y el destino.

Mi tiempo lo entregué sin villanías,
esas, tal vez se pudren bajo mi suerte,
no eché sobre otros hombros oscuros días,
ni entregué horas surtidas de muerte.

Mi tiempo lo atavié con la destreza
de hacerme fuerte donde otros temen,
y aun con la marca de insulsas perezas,
porque fue verano, tiempo me deben.

No pretendo cobrarle a Dios mi tiempo,
ni sangrarlo a hurtadilla de mi savia,
ni rentarlo con la mofa y con la rabia,
ni mostrarlo a estribor y a sotavento.

Solo quiero escribirlo con mi letra
como discurso urgido del intento,
que al margen del festín y la medra,
alguien, no lo dudo, me debe tiempo.

The Butterfly Lovers

Also the tragic love story of 梁山伯 *and* 祝英臺

by Chim Sher Ting

There was once a butterfly caught on the headstone between 9th and 20th boulevard. The young man with a pea-blossom coat touched it and it became an ampersand from a poem. The ampersand untangled itself from a sea of letters and it became a savannah, warm but disquieting like the arms of a lover. The savannah hadn't seen the arms of a lover in many years and it became a turntable, shuffling between two equally indifferent songs like a moth and the flickering garden torch. The moth talks about the Am, how it's both morning on the Amtrak and A minor, the saddest chord in history. A minor is the child bent over the headstone, not knowing that, twenty years later, he would ever release the butterfly. The butterfly is the moth is the colour we shower over our greatest disappointment. There was once a butterfly caught on the headstone between 9th and 20th boulevard. But the butterfly was long dead, and the boulevard only a young man's memory. You and you and you and me

Cuando la voz duerme y el corazón habla
by Tania Jasso Blancas

I

Anoche mentí con la sinceridad de un suicida,
escribí letras para encontrarte
atrapé el pasado entre los dientes
y el ruego en mi garganta estalló
ante mi propia espera.   Llegarás.
Abrí las ventanas y la puerta
de esta gran habitación que también fue tuya.
Espero   sentada frente a las palabras
que te esconden entre las esdrújulas
Aguardar,   y seguir aguantando resulta fácil
nunca estoy preparada, pero te espero
y al anochecer mentiré otra vez
con la sinceridad de un suicida.

II

Ocurrió que nos elevamos poco a poco y nos hundimos en la tierra,
ocurrió que nos hicimos gigantes,
y en los brazos nos salieron hojas
Nos quisimos en lo bello y lo salvaje
Nos recorrimos por dentro,   nos amamos por fuera
Imaginamos otro respirar,   imaginamos otro besar
          llegamos al cielo hundidos en la tierra
y no hay suelo que nos atrape,
Somos árbol buscando el río
con un par de ramas, bellas descendientes verdes
que bailan con el viento,   que ululan imponentes

Mentiremos sólo a quien nos cuestione
culparemos a aquella canción que nos habló
de otra forma de existir, de otra forma de resistir

Desde hoy, querido mío, somos árbol

MERGE

by Dee Allen

Desire for the miss from another race,
Still seems by some a total disgrace.
Environment and skin, different from mine.
Her shape, her heart—
Just causes for me
To cross over a phantom line.

She sees my colour and I see hers.
Black and White, in flesh made sacred, merge.
This century's norm—Sweeter wind, permissive this time—
Was a sin that led to the hangman's noose—
Last century's crime.

Andares
by Nelson Roque Pereira

> *Llegar allí es tu meta.*
> *Mas no apresures el viaje.*
> **Itaca. Kavafis.**

Un día dijeron que Itaca estaba
cerca de la ciudad del orden,
los álamos y las columnas.
Pero alguien decide los vientos
que desdobla el caminante
en rapto de los violines.

No importa la ruta o la fogata
si la madera se vivifica
cada amanecer, deslumbra,
entra un espejo en cada pecho,
y los brazos se nos tornan metas,
truenos en los senderos de estatuas.

Oh túmulo donde pernoctan los dioses!
Un día dijeron que Itaca estaba cerca,
allí donde los remos se aprestan al viaje,
y el sentido se desgrana en andares
como el picapedrero sobre la mañana,
dando forma permanente
al sudor en las manos del hombre.

Whispers from the womb
by Abubakar Auwal

Now mother has become a valley—
Of agony, anguish and durst of pestilence.
Her womb has turn to a hollow
Where evil of night
Cast their tales
And flaps their wings.
When she detected her brightness
The rays only hold
And behold in the evil's eyes.
From the back she reflect mirror of beauty
This smell odor of lined corpse
That never goes out of this pot they called cottage.
We keep whispering to brothers in reality
Yet, none discover the voice of baby children
As we keep circulating in the realms of anguish.
In this garden of hope and wishes
The poetic fluid overwhelmed a chatter
Of songs flowing from the dyke of our spittles
Now the sound of our screaming
Had rise to bleed out
And beat the drums of merciful doctor
Then the tears of our first day should
Water a good father to freeze this mother.

Renacer del Ave Fénix
por Bertha Galán

Permanecí como un árbol seco en agonía
sin raíces, sin hojas, sin flores,
tocó en mí, la antorcha mortecina y vaga
de un anochecido cielo sin nubes al vacío,
marchitando la faz de mis ojos en hiel.
***
Una mañana grácil de abril, desperté con
la suave lluvia…
        descendía entre mis hojas vespertinas la luz,
        coreados con el plácido viento, y con su brío
tocó su fuerza en mí.
***
El sol abrazó mi sombra con redención,
la tormenta gris, huyó de mi camino
mis alas rotas renovaron el vuelo mágico
del águila en su júbilo.
***
Ahora mis alas gozan de audacia,
con la fortaleza del mar y el sol,
resurgí como el ave fénix desde las cenizas,
entonces comprendí…
¡que el universo lo llevaba dentro!

The Probable Absurdity of Our Existence
by Christopher T. Dabrowski

What if our expanding universe is a cell of a vast organism of limited quantity in a growth phase?

If so, we are facing extinction at some point. Unless we somehow save ourselves.

And if we manage to grow enough to spread through the universe and learn to get into the next ones, are we by chance something like a spreading disease?

And if, having reached the bordering universe, we get outside this huge body, will we accidentally be the cause of another pandemic in our host world?

Hmm... Maybe it's better to sit on Earth waiting for the end.

Luces de neón
por Yonnier Torres Rodríguez

1

A mediodía el sol se traga los colores de esta Isla\ Nos devuelve la mugre\ El pensamiento embotado\ El desatino de cubrir los cristales con recortes de revistas.

Mi madre taponea los agujeros para que el resplandor no se trague las baldosas\ Con anuncios de cosméticos forra las persianas para que la claridad no muerda los cuadros en la pared\ los retratos de los quince de mi hermana\ el diploma enmarcado como sobras de un concurso literario.

Mi padre envuelve la puerta en papel periódico para que la luz no mastique los recuerdos.

2

A mediodía el sol se traga los colores de esta Isla\ Nos devuelve brochazos grises sobre el asfalto\ las columnas\ la gente\ Borra los contornos de los edificios\ las gárgolas\ las cornisas\ Afronta el filo de las antenas que sostienen el cielo.

3

A mediodía el sol se traga los colores de esta Isla\ Poco a poco\ nos vamos acostumbrando a la oscuridad.

Unfold My Heart
by Tabassum Tahmina Shagufta Hussein

Unfold my heart,
O love, of my inner being.
Make it pure,make it luminous.
Make it immaculate.
Rouse from slumber,
Lift it high
Free it from fear,
Bless me,
Make me diligent,
Remove all my doubts.
Unite me with all around.
Free me from all chains.
May Thy gentle melody
Bless everything I do.
May my soul stay unmoved,
Bless me with Thy lotus feet
With joy,with peace and with happiness.

Mi gesto
por Santiago Domínguez

Mi gesto es la palabra
la palabra roja
que sangra del pápel.

Mi gesto es la palabra
la palabra naranja
que lleva el ácido a las gargantas.

Mi gesto es la palabra
la palabra amarilla
que hace parpadear al sol.

Mi gesto es la palabra
la palabra verde
que en los domingos el otoño extraña.

Mi gesto es la palabra
la palabra celeste
que separa al mar del cielo.

Mi gesto es la palabra
la palabra azul
que usa como espejo hasta el agua.

Mi gesto es la palabra
la palabra violeta
que colorea ese momento esperado entre diciembre y enero.

Mi gesto es la palabra
que antes de ser palabra
se maquila con el arcoíris.

THIS INEXPLICABLE NEED
by Edward Lee

The silence you left
comforts me
more than your voice
ever did, or your touch,
or, for that matter,
your very presence,
my existence one of constantly coiled apprehension
that I might disappoint you,
anger you,
lose you,

all of which I did,
and more, but
that is not why you are gone;

your heart simply ceased,
quickly, surprisingly.
Your heart ceased
and now you are gone.

I miss you,
without missing you,
the comfort of silence,
the absence of the fear
of angering you,
not enough
to calm my need for you
beside me, this inexplicable need

EL GRITO
por Rodrigo Miguel Quintero

Tiré las cosas alrededor, humo denso,
hoy era el día, era su aniversario.
Las mariposas en el ombligo se ahogaron
en falsos juramentos, muecas quebradizas, sombras,
la cara del silencio, torcida, reventada.
Se me erizaron, de pronto, los pelos de la nuca.
Llegó el frío, la oscuridad, el mundo...
¡sin mí, sin ella, sin nosotros!
Nuestras angustias descalzas de ilusiones,
desnudas como un niño.
El Dios del humo acogotando el aire,
riéndose descalzo y la muerte, acechando.

INSENSITIVITY, 'THE FALL' AND ZEN MONASTERIES
by Douglas Colston

Pouring insensitivity
assembles
neglect, suppression, indulgence, secrecy and gloom …
the vessel 'falsehood and illegitimacy'
conveying descent
that some might consider
akin to falling in love with a prostitute –
it is a shipwreck
wearing a disguise
appearing otherwise innocuous
like a Zen monastery or a thicket.

Identidad Desconocida
por Miriam Romero

Where are you from?
I mean, you have a beautiful accent… but I can't tell what you are?

Who am I? What am I?
Preguntas frecuentes que no logro responder

Are you from India?
Are you from the Middle East?
¿Eres de Colombia? suenas como colombiana.
Cuando te vi pensé que eras de… pero te escuché, eres de México, ¿verdad?

Who am I? What am I?
Preguntas frecuentes que no logro responder

¿Quién soy? ¿Qué soy?
Soy mestiza,
Soy una mezcla de culturas, razas y colores

I am US citizen porque nací en los Estados Unidos But I don't look "American"
Soy mexicana por herencia de mis padres
Buy you don't look "Mexican"
Soy Tejana por que nací, crecí y viví en Tejas
Pero no llevo botas ni sombrero
Soy fronteriza porque crecí en la frontera.
Pero la frontera no se te nota…

I am someone who's constantly connected with something. I am unknown.
Adoptó la identidad que se requiere en el momento o el lugar. I am someone
without an identity.

I am borderless… *identityless*… I am, just I am.

Florecer
por Estrella Gracia González

Anhelé ascender al cielo
sobre desiertos espinosos y ríos de congoja
en mi pretensión de olvidar.

Liviano es el sentimiento y acero las
palabras
que se ahogan en pantanos
de soledad.

Promesas plasmadas en lienzo
como bocetos
sin color.

Ha desaparecido el brillo de sus ojos
dejando frío en la carne
y un reloj en el infierno se derrite.

Mi luto lo acompañaron los cuervos,
sembré mi corazón con lágrimas.

Hoy protejo el retoño
en espera de que un día
florezcan palomas blancas.

KILCOLMAN

by Anita Howard

Dwarfed by whispering crops,
we staged our reinvasion
of half-felled curtain wall
and tower built to see for miles -
survivors of two burnings.

In early evening sunlight,
communion felt easy.
How neatly threads were woven!
Knights, shepherds and Greek gods
repopulating, stroke by righteous stroke,
these lands of plenty:
unstoppable sprawl
of interloper's mythology.
And as we moved away,
squat walls bound up with ivy
breathed near-farewell.
But deeper truths breathed too.
I woke that night, heart pounding
and worlds bleak in my mind,
to know, at last, the fire in those fields -
forever trespasser in their loom of darkness.

EL ERRANTE
por Rolando Reyes López

Justo antes que el tiempo tuviera lenguaje propio;
cuando el rito y la herejía
se disputaban la creación del hombre;
durante la guerra entre la luz y la ceguera,
como una ambición apresurada del destino;
de la estirpe de Dios y del soldado;
del aliento de una boca con argumentos;
erigido donde sucede la noche
necesaria y conclusiva;
después de lo que viene y se abre frente al árbol,
sin murallas que lo separen de la roca
o de la puesta de sol;
impreso en las nubes, en el asfalto,
en la cumbre del sueño mismo,
en lo que empieza y termina,
el errante que salió de los hielos azules
entra a la ciudad, cruza el río
y pasa.

Youngblood en la Frontera
by William David

Let me go from the hell new dawn creates.
My eyes ever visit the cheerful hideaways.

If I need visit the hangman's hideaway
and my virtues are counted as sins so be it.

But I'm already judged no need
for a courthouse or jail cell.

Then let me go. I am labeled an outlaw.
My only crime was living a life

in defiance of greed and corrupt laws.
I stole to feed the starving

to comfort the sick. So hurry at least
I'll have my dignity not like your kind.

Death in your dull old age.
Not living while you're alive, aye?

Hurry you dogs and let Death settle my debt.
You'll be settling yours soon enough.

La constelación de los dos amantes
por Gabriel González Núñez

La larga noche es un manto turquesa
que en la inmensidad se estira tirante.
Nada escapa a la hondura de su sombra
que empapa todo de matices quietos.
Lejanas refulgen pepitas de oro
que danzan timoratas en el cielo.

Ahora la superficie marina
parece hecha de trémula obsidiana.
Nuestro barco va cortando las aguas
con su proa silente y de metal.
Un búho se posa sobre el timón
y una brisa suave impulsa la vela.

Tus pupilas del color del café
recorren inquietas la lejanía.
Nos cruzamos las miradas de cómplices
que navegan el misterio nocturno.
La mano bajo y dejo que las yemas
de los dedos rocen el agua fresca.

Hace muchos años ya que zarpamos
de aquel puerto de casitas de cristal.
A nuestras espaldas se hundió la costa
y aún no vemos el filo del mundo.
Un día a esa cascada llegaremos
y esto entonces sucederá, mi amada:

Unas grandes alas de cisne tierno
nuestro barco al infinito alzarán.
Las estrellas cabida nos darán
en su morada de sosiego eterno.

Y no habrá constelación más brillante
que la nuestra, la de los dos amantes.

Inside out I see
by Olivier Pascalin

Observing my life from inside
The truth is that I am amazed
It's not that I wanted to change it
But if you highlight how much to love

Inside out I see
Sometimes I see a lot of what is not seen
See it as you want I worry
From so many wrong looks

Precisely for all that
I would like not to see and blindly
Behave lovingly
They do not know how happy I am

I would like to share nothing more of that
And even more before leaving
I did not tell them goodbye
But anyway if even life

Migrante
por Chepy Salinas Domínguez

Camino al sueño americano
cargas   ilusiones
y tus pies cansados
sigues bajo el solo deseo de cruzar al país de ensueño,
donde los niños matan,
el color de piel te condena
 y la vida es salvaje
 La jaula de oro
Migrante, hoy ya en caravanas
desfilan a las fronteras
Necesidad   Necedad
        pobreza.   Mal gobierno
           Frontera.   Muerte
vicios   Delincuencia   Muerte
          Adiós migrante

Love Like Tacos
by Juan Manuel Perez

think of tacos when you're thinking of me
how soft my tortilla or hard my shell
how everything I am gives a good smell

think of tacos when you're thinking of me
how warm my skin and delicious my heart
how I hold on without falling apart

think of tacos when you're thinking of me
how my spices ignite all your senses
how nothing from me marks up expenses

think of tacos when you're thinking of me
how I make you smile, delight your hunger
be a good salsa, please call my number

Una plegaria más
por José Luis Moreno

Los rieles que se pierden silenciosos
se han llevado la paz de nuestra vista
y se escapan los sueños presurosos
Por el sueño de un hombre y su conquista...

Un niño en el silencio recitaba
unas plegarias que le daban sueño.
Yo, lo miraba, triste, y me sentaba...
Él, es Oscar, mi niño más pequeño.

Después me preguntaba por el cielo
y por la virgen pura y bondadosa.
Le hablaba de su amor y su consuelo
ya que el alma de ella es generosa.

Entonces me pregunta soñoliento
¿Por qué la paz se fue de nuestra tierra?
Y otro murmullo me quitó el aliento
¿Por qué los niños marchan a la guerra?

Le dije duerme, con un beso plugo
y sueña que cabalgas un caballo
deja que Dios se vuelva su verdugo,
suspiro, y luego, callo... solo callo.

Es mi silencio del que más reniego,
mientras sueña sus sueños infantiles
otro a su edad, está gritando ¡fuego!
atrincherado en miedos y fusiles…

La triste realidad que nos oprime,
la busco con razón desesperada.
Le pido a Dios... a nuestro Dios sublime
y en el silencio no me dice nada.

Las horas pasan entre notas graves
y de las veladoras, por sus luces,
se ven fantasmas que parecen aves
de tanto niño que quedó sin cruces.

Y miro en el silencio sus dolores
 y siento la bondad en su ignorancia
vivieron de la guerra sus horrores
la sabia patria se tragó su infancia.

En esa procesión, sin sus pendones,
miré sus tristes sombras en desvelo
murieron por las balas y cañones,
¿Acaso por honor se gana el cielo?

Y despierta mi niño, y me entristece,
al decirme: no temas... solo eso
y al olvido de aquello que enardece
me deja por mi frente un dulce beso.

La respuesta de Dios que yo quería
en lágrimas de fe por la bonanza,
como tren de la paz y la alegría
regresa con un beso en esperanza.

My Chest was Like the Coconut
by Stephen Douglas Wright

My chest was like the coconut
I split on the big beach rock
Whose broken cavity, wispy tendrils
Would birth and feed a fire

But the coconut was dry
And I, not a coconut,
But only like the coconut,
Could not be contained, broke open

My wet essence poured out through
my chest
My hands could not catch myself
I, not a coconut, but a jack-o-lantern
Spewed insides out

Overflowing with thoughts of you,
Two sets of eyes entangled
Quantum mirror-dancing in our ocean irises
Two sets of breath rising like suns,
falling like stars

I, twisted tooth pumpkin
Sliced up, down and sideways
Shaded from sun on the concrete porch
Recalling cold knife, warm scooping hands

What am I to do
Your memory twisting its vines,
spared pumpkin seed?
What am I to do
With my insides out?

Sweet coconut milk and blood
Run down and through my fingers
All that was in me now soaks in the Earth
And I, now dry as the coconut,
might feed a fire

A veces quiero dejar de escribir
por Roswel Borges Castellanos

entrar a una discoteca
y bailar hasta que me duelan las costillas
A veces quisiera
dejar de sembrar mariposas
ignorar las azucenas
los girasoles
volver a recuperar las paredes
el techo
el suelo que una vez perdí
que ya no encuentro
que ya no existen
A veces envidio a esos jóvenes que bailan
que no piensan
que guiñen el ojo a la chica
y logran conquistarlas irreductiblemente
sin pensar y sin pedir nada a cambio
solamente con un diente de oro
o dos
o tres
A veces quisiera
dejar de ser yo
de buscarte para volar
A veces quisiera dejar de escribir
pero no puedo
vuelvo a encontrarme nuevamente
con una hoja en blanco
buscando tu nombre

Cafuné
by Nancy Jo Allen

is the Portuguese word
for becoming tangled
in a lover's hair.
That very action
may also disentangle
silky strands of feeling
beyond that comforting tickle.
It creates a cocoon
that says:
become something new,
and beautiful with me.

FINAL Y PRINCIPIO

por Wendy B. Lara

Recordando aquel momento que nos dimos un sí.
Un sí, que duraría toda la vida.
Toda la vida tuya o toda la vida mía.
La vida mía que no contaba los segundos del reloj.
Del reloj que ahora no importa lo que marca.
Marca que dejaron tus besos en mi piel.
Mi piel que ahora está marchita y fría.
Fría como cada noche en que tu calor me cobijaba.
Me cobijaba con el calor de tu amor.
Tu amor es lo único que recuerdo en este pequeño espacio.
Espacio que ya no tengo en el mundo.
El mundo que me pertenecía.
Me pertenecía la vida, sus emociones y alegrías.
Alegrías y también las tristezas.
Las tristezas que ahora te dejo.
Ahora te dejo sin mí porque ya he muerto.

Provenance Of My Rage
by Megha Sood

A sudden gush of emotions
that slowly traverses—
rising up like scorched mercury
through knots of my undulating spine

An unsettling notion of standing
a little too close to the kiln
my emotions rise and reach the crescendo
simmering and brimming to the core

Words are failing to form at the mouth
falling incessantly to their untimely death
mumbling and gnashing teeth—
spitting truth in between

Here the veracity of my truth depends
on the color of my skin
and the exalted Gods in heaven
To those, I pray with my folded hands

This unsettling feeling of fear and orphan rage
I feel under my walnut skin,
as I walk on the empty streets in the morning
fighting the loneliness and the voiceless din

Confronted by a stranger's voice
that sends shivers to my bone
laced with privilege passed to him for generations
with his blue blood coursing through his veins

A country he boisterously calls home
asking me with the sheer audacity
with his forked tongue and in his vile voice
hurling insults wrapped in his privilege
to go back,
to where I belong.

Migajas de paraíso
por Felix Cardoso

Mar, he caminado día y noche porque el viento me arrastró a tus brazos; seguí a estrellas iluminadoras de tus bramidos, seguí tu fragancia de lágrimas hasta el horizonte preñado y ruborizado; donde la arena se incrustó entre mis dedos. Ahí, tendiste un mantel de bienvenida y desvaneciste la nieve de mis anteriores pasos, hiciste cosquillas en mi piel, en el pelo, en mi mente; acariciaste a mis demonios en los escalones de infinitas luciérnagas y tímida bruma, creaste sonidos que suenan a sueños rebeldes, a latidos que no dejan de suspirar.

Pude saltar en tus olas y beber los inciensos de tus crepúsculos, de tu silencio o ruido de tus latidos graznando; la misma voz que no teme la muerte por eso brama por eso guarda migajas de paraíso y se petrifica en letanías que conocieron a los ancianos, los mismos que pusieron mis ojos en la senda de eternos besos.

Mar, hueles a misterio enrojecido a caricias que no dejan de sudar, a cuerpo que transmuta en águilas o jaguares de espiritual acústica, a leyendas que hipnotizan al relámpago y a la lluvia, a dulce *atecocolli* que hace danzar a tus olas, y a tus hijos que flotan en blanca espuma. Humedeces de sabiduría a los cuerpos, los de arena renovada a cada suspiro, los que aprendieron a percibir y buscar sus alimentos en marea alta, los que se tatuaron a orión a porque son hermanos de las estrellas y a ellas les cantan y a ellas iluminan con sus actos de amor y sacrificios.

Cada segundo siento a la hermana muerte respirar en la sal que mastica a mis labios, pero he llegado al lugar donde el agua grande refleja mi rostro de cabellos alborotados, donde los ancianos de piel tostada curaban ataduras de maíz y frijol, y las iguanas con su arcoíris incluido siguen lamiendo cicatrices, y en este paraíso, no escucho más a la hermana muerte.

RETURN TO THE VALLEY
by Margaret Cantu-Sanchez

Our trips to The Rio Grande Valley are
woven into my mind and body.
Both intuitively know the way
as if the spirits of my grandparents are calling me back.

From San Antonio…281/37 South.
The roads are lined---
ranches, cattle, horses, maíz and---rows of billowy cotton made stiff in the
hot Texas sun.

We pass by and through small towns.
Pleasanton, Whitsett, Three Rivers.
Robstown, the halfway point.

All the towns named after people,
gringos and Mexicanos alike.
Alice, Kingsville, Ricardo, Sarita, Raymondville.

Small towns,
ranching and farming communities.
The people, languages, and radio stations shift here.

Mexicanos, Mexican Americans, Tejanos, and winter Texans.
English becomes Spanish, Spanglish, and Tex-Mex.
Music transforms into Conjunto, Tejano, and cumbias.

The landscape signals a change as well.
Ranches littered with green, prickly nopales,
scratchy brush, and tall palm trees line the center median
reaching their palms to heaven.

The weather too beckons a constant, swirly wind.
Dry and warm, it directs the tall grass and palms like a conductor of a symphony.

Some would have you believe the Valley is only a place of…
violence, corruption, and poverty.

But I know better.
In the Valley, my past and family resides.
It is where I learned about myself, my future, and the place to which I will
always return.

Baijiu/ Wong Fei vuelve a casa
por José Rodolfo Espinosa Silva

El sol descendente riega colores,
rojo y rosado con una pizca de naranja;
la luz baña las tejas curvas de los hogares
cuyos aleros anchos crean una sombra
que se proyecta a varios metros.

Wong Fei no es diestro en el amor, Baijiu lo sabe muy bien,
con su elixir le alivia las penas, lo hace bravo y decidido.
Empuja a Wong Fei hacia una joven, una sonrisa y un beso etílico,
Wong Fei abandona la taberna con la brisa fresca que anuncia la noche,
géiseres en el estómago, pasos tambaleantes
y Baijiu alegre le mueve el suelo.

El grito de un hombre hostil lo alcanza:
¡besaste a mi chica!
nace un círculo de morbo alrededor de ellos,
Baijiu danza alegre, le emocionan los combates.
El agresor se aproxima
con ceja arrugada y puños cerrados.
Wong Fei da un trago a su cantimplora,
garganta de dragón, postura de tigre,
patada sin destino,
Baijiu lo cuida
lo hace caer.
Wong Fei se para en un salto,
*ojo de fénix**, copa invisible,
estilo del mono,
golpe, patada, caída, ambos en el suelo,
sólo Wong Fei se levanta.

Cuando la luna toma el lugar del sol,
Wong Fei vuelve a casa.

*La forma de borracho utiliza el puño "ojo de fénix" en la mano que sujeta la imaginaria copa de
  vino y se hace golpeando con el nudillo del dedo índice.

DESIRE
by Aldo Cristian Méndez Castillo

I'm thinking about you,
way beyond my dreams.
filled with lust and love,
fantasy going through my soul.

Your taste lies inside me,
the beauty of your body.
a desire grows wildly in my heart,
kind of sexual bright, that I like…

Thinking of you, as I did before,
while my words touch this paper,
my heart keep dreaming of us,
remembering that sweet september.

I want you again and again,
I don't mind letting loose all I've got.
if you don't leave this room,
I will be with you, until the end.

Escape

por Irlyan del Carmen Hernández Sosa de Bacalar

Corriendo,
me preguntaba
¿De quién huía?
¿A quién temía?
Pero recordé
que a la muerte
nadie escapa.
Sonreí.
porque la
realidad me golpeó,
me hizo darme
cuenta que no
podía huir,
huir de mis demonios,
ni de lo que yo
misma había provocado.
Porque ya no había
salida,
no había un cuerpo
que pudiera salir
de aquel ruin
lugar, porque
él ya había
disparado y mi
alma era la que
observaba.

MULTI-STOREYED

by Sharanya B

Flat 2G: A middle-aged woman pleads her visiting son to divorce his "*disobedient*" wife
She narrates the wonderful plans calculated for his future
As meticulously as the high-school math she taught for many decades
"The gold was less, the land is not enough,
The woman's arrogant, you deserve better, just end this."

1A: The pensioned couple skim again for the hundredth time
Through visas, passports and all the necessary documents
Their packed and arranged baggage waiting at the foyer
The wife zips up the last bag holding pickles, *papads*
And all the desi sweets their NRI grandchildren crave

2B: An IT professional has just been credited his monthly payment
In the comfort of solitude
He twists open a brand-new whiskey bottle
And curls up in the couch with a lighted cigarette
Spiraling into a meditation bound to last for eternity

3A: A nonchalant teenager pulls out her grade-sheet
From the deck of unmaintained notebooks resting on a postered table
An angry father awaits and a curious mother busy in the kitchen
Prepares her warning speech:
"Nothing can save you if not for education."

4A: The tired manager is back from her work,
With an approved maternity leave
She gulps down cold water from the fridge,
Barely standing in her third trimestered belly
Impatient to land on the cushioned bed and stretch her back
Video call the husband and work on baby names

HIGHER ABOVE: A vast and purple sky, soon dimming
Silhouettes of birds flitting by in a rush
The sun patiently sinks into the horizon
As another world eagerly awaits its share of daylight

Astrología
por Ana Saldaña

Si creyera en la astrología
pensaría que tiene alguna relevancia cósmica
no querer levantarme los viernes,
leer hasta tarde en la cama,
no dormir si bebo café después de las siete.
Pensaría que son cualidades intrínsecas
de las mujeres que nacimos
poco antes de la primavera,
en el punto más cálido
del invierno, como un tubérculo
liberándose de su capullo de tierra
después de hibernar por meses.

Gone Shopping
by Allan Lake

Climate chaos has already tipped
many into uncertainty but bright
sales at the factory outlets have
certainly captured my attention.
Discount dreaming as flames
and water wave goodbye,
goodbuy.

no te nombro

por Alejandro Zapata Espinosa

no te nombro
porque sería acompañar mi soledad
y ya está bien con que la hayas provocado

The Poor Man
by Binod Dawadi

I am the poor man,
Who loves and cares for me ?
I have nothing,
I am orphan,
My parents throws me in the road,
I search food and eat there,

I don't have education,
I don't have works,
Everybody hates and dominates me,
I am very much disappointed,
No body rubs my pains,
I am the poor man.

Como el viento
por Ramiro Hernández Restrepo

Como el viento
revolviendo hojas
por si acaso un verso.

Something Long Gone
by Candace Meredith

Laps of water
Thick as butter

Doorbells don't chime
Rustic in color

Scented of ancient
Times newspaper

An archaic moon
Against the new sun

In the shadow of destiny
Upon the wall a clock

Marching toward dinner
Aloft a metal frame bunk bed

Is a straw stuffed mattress
In the cottage of steel-toed

Work boots to pay homage
To the mining shafts

They fill their plates of copper
And the silver dollars they find

Too many to go around
There are still empty stomachs

In the contrasts of smelling colors
They visualize the scent of something

Long gone.

CUANDO NO ME MIRAS
por Víctor Hugo Orduña Silguero

Saturno no avanza cuando no me miras,
las cosas cambian de sitio de forma inoportuna,
las estrellas se ponen tristes,
y los dioses se cansan de jugar a la creación.

Donde ayer hubo un árbol,
hoy silencios
monocromáticos hay.
Donde ayer un camino,
hoy páginas en blanco.
Donde ayer un ayer,
un manglar de fantásticos recuerdos.

Lo mismo pasa con las personas, los relojes y las cucharas,
los perros van desprendiendo su ladridos
cada día un tanto más.
Si se oye un maullido, son las nostalgias que
disfrazadas de quehaceres tratan de contradecir al viento.

Las cosas pierden su sabor e identidad
                    y da lo mismo nombrar
al vaso por   jirafa,
al elefante por sombrero,
                    al frío
por escopeta
y a la nostalgia por vanidad.

En tu presencia gravita una sintaxis jamás nombrada,
eres
un
invento
gramatical
subterráneo.

Si fraseo tu imagen se reprograman los c r e p ú s c u l o s,
si tararareo tu esencia se descuelgan los cálidos rojos del t i e m p o.

Los objetos caen hacia arriba

                                                        cuando no me miras,
                              y entonces brillan las oscuridades, oscuran los brillos,
aturden los silencios, silencian las aturdos,
mojan los fuegos, fuegan los mojos,
queman las lluvias, lluvian los quemos,
encienden los fríos y frían los enciendos.

Las vocales son números y con cifras se escriben las carcajadas,
da igual ser hombre o cicatriz de un sol olvidado,
raspón en la esquina de un suspirar
o pájaro en fingido vuelo.

Da lo mismo estar o no ser,
reír que soñar,
lo mismo da, alto que rojo, vacío que cielo,
vivo que quiero, necio que luna,
carro que niño, pato que enero.

Si arranco la fruta del naranjo, en realidad me estoy atando las agujetas.
Si mastico un bocado, en realidad me estoy afeitando las lágrimas.
Si veo televisión, la verdad es que grito tu nombre escondido.

Hay otros mundos detrás de mil no me miras y en este preciso momento
escucho las nubes nadar en reversa mientras pienso:

                        ¿A dónde voy,
            de dónde vengo, cuál es mi verdadera equivalencia,
                  mi rostro, mi equidistancia etérea?

                        Tal vez
              en el reflejo en tus ojos
                  lo encuentro
                  me encuentro

lo entiendo.

Sundays
by E. Martin Pedersen

Sunday mornings are quiet on the rocks
pika cries are swept off by the wind
it's always windy
the clouds are hopping
showing off their weekend dance moves
they come out like gophers
on the high school soccer field
then about noon they run off like lemmings
run in circles like hamsters
on the wheel of progress
wheel of fortune, wheel within a wheel
spinning inside / out
on Sundays
I've looked
at clouds

Adagio sognante
por Eduardo Omar Honey Escandón

dormía infinito conectado
al largo adiós de la condena
el silencio vestido con sombras
abrumadoras me opacaba

ensordecedores ruidos abismales
explotaron en el firmamento
rompiendo los sellos del ocaso
convirtiendo el sepulcro

tu rostro, mi esperanza, de la sima
surgió expulsando al mar onírico
desde la noche cósmica me nombró
con un "¿me recuerdas?"

memorias del futuro en este no-lugar
ondularon con las brisas estelares
supe que eras mi primer aliento
después del coma sin esperanza

Non places
by Jackie Kabir

We met at non places
You and I,
Where there is uncertainty
Where there is ephemerality
Where there is no center
Frantically we tried to find a ground
Fervently we looked for an anchorage
straddling between home and non-home
Oscillating between belonging and non-belonging.
Moving between dreams and reality.
Between imagination and rock-solid actuality.
Now places have become non-places
Homes have become non-homes.
You and I have become non-acquainted.

Lenguaje milenario
por Alejandro Chang Hernández

Odas escritas por poetas
En los caminos y las plazas
A lo largo de la historia.

Canciones que tejen almas
Encontrando en parajes escondidos
La magia de un beso alado.

Emociones que inundan de luz clara
En las noches oscuras del hastío
Los corazones que aman sin palabras.

Riqueza eterna que provoca
La magia que llena la mirada
Y las más secretas ilusiones.

Belleza eterna que compone
Versos extraños y candentes,
Guardianes fieles de los hombres.

Lenguaje que grita en el silencio
Las más secretas confesiones,
Herederas de gloriosos sentimientos.

This is not a poem
by Roxana Arroyo

This

is a blinding shot of light blue.

This is your first breath,
the first time you held
another's hand. This is
tiny toes and cozy cheeks.

This is the clothes you
wore every day,
those huge pockets in which
you carried your greatest years
and your biggest dreams.

This is every person who
ever loved you.

This is a white gown,
our thinned voices,
the last time you held
my hand. This is
the empty, recently made
bed.

This is a blinding shot of light blue,

an abstraction of time.

This is the moment you were born and
the moment you died.

FELIS POETRIS CATUS
por G. Libedinsky

Yo soy un Gato.
Lo descubro cuando me escabullo
al Horizonte Nocturno de la Existencia…

Pero sucede que a veces debo vestirme de Humana
para salir a la Vida;
es en los Días que mis pupilas se agrandan
y desconocen la Noche;
es en las Horas Mortales que caminó Erguida
y oculto mis Garras.

Y nadie advierte que no soy Humana.
Yo me aíslo del Mundo y sus Luces,
yazgo en mi Esfera de Sombras Eternas
donde reposan las Auras Obscuras…

Yo soy un Gato.
Yo observo Tinieblas y Espectros danzantes,
la Gris realidad que habita este Plano.

Pero sucede que las personas me miran
y sólo ven a Gabriela;
la Mujer depresiva, la Poeta Suicida.
Ellos me piensan soy la Loca Escriba;
una Mina cualquiera…

Ya que sus Ojos se posan ausentes
cuando les enseño mi Alma.
Se mantienen ignaros a la Verdad de mi Estrella
que obscurece a mi Manto y les revela mi Esencia…

Puesto y yo soy un Gato.
Yo no habito esta Piedra que los Humanos corroen.
Yo me divago en los Reinos que ellos jamás han soñado.

FELIS POETRIS CATUS
by G. Libedinsky

I am a Cat.
I find out when I slip away
to the Night Horizon of Existence…

But it happens that sometimes I must dress as a Human
to go out to Life;
it is on the days that my pupils get bigger
and they do not know the Night;
it is in the Deadly Hours that I walk upright
and hide my Claws.

And no one notices that I'm not Human.
I isolate myself from the World and their Lights,
I lie in my Sphere of Eternal Shadows
where the Dark Auras rest…

I am a Cat.
I observe Darkness and dancing Specters,
the Gray reality that inhabits this Plane.

But it happens that people look at me
and they only see Gabriela;
the depressive Woman, the Suicidal Poet.
They think I'm the Crazy Scribe;
any woman like others…

Since their eyes rest absently
when I show them my Soul.
They remain ignorant of the Truth of my Star
that obscures my Mantle and reveals my Essence…

Since I am a Cat.
I do not inhabit this Stone that Humans corrode.
I wander in the Kingdoms that they have never dreamed of.

MIS OJOS HECHIZAN
por Claudia Elisa Saquicela Novillo

YMis labios cantan en vez de tragar,
mis manos lavan almas en vez de romperlas,
mis ojos hechizan en vez de llorar.

Mi vida dejó de dolerme,
justo cuando mi alma cosecha jazmines,
mis ojos hechizan en vez de que
mi vientre sonríe en vez de ocultar,
mis brazos crean en vez de matar.

Mis ojos hechizan en vez de amar
¡Mis dedos caminan para llegar al final!
mi lengua perfuma con palabras las tardes blancas,
mis costillas aman en vez de asfixiar.

Mis dientes hablan en vez de morder,
mi nariz piensa en vez de infectar.
hoy ya no lloro, solo renazco en una flor
y mis ojos no paran de hechizar a todos.

The Line Between
by Thomas Ray Garcia

wait for the man in the mirror to move
and don't follow — it's what they think you'll do
when your body is caught on the line

watch him like the weight of the country's gaze
bending our eyes to the scars we hide inside —
there are no open wounds on our bodies

only on what's remembered and what is —
elisions of landscapes trouble my sight
and fragment the line between

    this road I remember was already paved
        these patrol trucks never took up space
            those sunglass eyes hiding lies

            looking is a complicated thing
        it makes a watcher out of time
    the sites passing away, no memory

the voices on screens talking, talking
        talking to myself across the looking glass
            will never change the border like they do —

        if I lie, the dying's over. but if
    I die, the lying lives. I realize
the man in the mirror never dies

ashé andino
por Enrique Manuel Infante Ángeles

Wiracocha
me protege y guía
visitó el pacífico de Pachacamac
      y nado con mis pies congelados en fuego
      de tanto andar mientras que con mirada azuzada
Inti
      me arma de valor para seguir mis caminos
      voy a las montañas mi alma visita su
Apu
      en mi búsqueda por conectar con el
Hanan Pacha
      que oxigena mis pulmones
Pachamama
      me anida en su centro
      me hago paso en la amazonía
      un chamán señala mi oriente
      pues toda orientación debe empezar por el este
      dejo mi
Kay Pacha
      por instantes luz y cuando me enfrento con mi
Uku Pacha
      entiendo un poco más el porqué de mis
      trepida   iones
Illapa   Mama Cocha   Mama Sara y Mama Quilla están
      pendientes de su hijo

Aurora Borealis Teach Me To Utter *I Love You*
by Kim Malinowski

I wished for so many stars.
I galloped mountains back, forth
cracked rock like lichen
no love potion strong enough to bridge chasm.
We say *friend* as if this road
could wash out by hurricane.
As if snow could smother dreams
if we let it.
I want my stars coated with love
swirl of colors in northern skies.
I beg my body by trowel and shovel.
Teach me strength.
Teach me trust.
There is fear that wars with my recklessness
anxiety that knows calamity
knows you might swamp the bridge yourself
if careless and my heart, if careless.
Strangers tell me that poetry cannot win wars.
Poetry cannot bring in dough.
I fold poetry into dough, batter, tell the oven
my winter wants, breathe in my magic potion.
Elixirs come, go.
Poetry stays scribbled in corners
like spiders, hides torn emotions, those scary, fierce, words
I cannot utter even to the gods.
Teach us the word *together*. Let us be careless.
We will bridge chasm, chasing snow dreams with burning lights.
Poetry does win wars,
that means our battle will end with soft
lilac and grassy skies.

LO QUE FUI, LO QUE SOY
por Baltazar Cordero Tamez

Soy lo que fui,
cosecha del mejor de mis aciertos,
consecuencia también de mis errores
en el incierto andar de mi destino
con la brújula correcta del camino

Soy lo que soy,
lección aprendida en el destiempo,
lámpara que asoma a mi ventana
para hacer más firme el paso donde encuentro
verdades y mentiras en concierto.

Soy lo que fui, soy lo que soy,
crisol de amores y esperanzas,
y conciencia del dolor que orando alcanzas.
Soy lo que ves, lo que respiro
felicidad entre los versos donde estoy,
dialogando en el espejo
que nunca miente
y siempre alumbra el camino
lleno de luz por donde voy.

Behold The Raging River
by Dorthy LaVern Spencer McCarthy

The old, Red River rages on its way
in waves, uncounted miles of mud and sand.
It was a timid stream just yesterday
before the rains arrived and took command.
In waves, uncounted miles of mud and sand,
it surges to the Gulf of Mexico.
Before the rains arrived and took command,
the river was a gentle lamb, and slow.

It surges to the Gulf of Mexico
from Palo Duro, its beginning place.
The river was a gentle lamb, and slow
with skies of April mirrored on its face.
From Palo Duro, its beginning place,
it gains momentum, whirling on and on,
with skies of April mirrored on its face
now cold and dark, with beauty, dead and gone.

It gains momentum, whirling on and on,
a demon none can tame forever more.
Now cold and dark, with beauty, dead and gone,
it plunges on to reach a peaceful shore.
A demon none can tame forever more,
it was a timid stream just yesterday.
It plunges on, to reach a peaceful shore.
The old Red River rages on its way.

Changüí
por Iván Medina

Campesino de piel curtida
por el aire de esta vida,
 pregona a la tierra,
 a tu Cecilia guajira.
Ara a la madre labriego
 fecundando su interior
con azadón, semilla y sudor.
Pizca el fruto de tu entrega,
con alegría; canto que llega.
Campestre beodo
por el néctar de la caña
del hijo de tu entraña,
 sin bohío, pero esperanza.
Pulula libre por el monte guajiro,
entre la trémula mata ciguaraya
que exhala el verano
 donde el aire invisible es puro y claro.
Contempla la quietud
 del árbol que se eleva
con magnífico esplendor
en este tupido jardín
donde quema el brusco sol
 que es la Sierra Maestra.

Luz de estrellas
por Antonio Ramírez Córdova

En tu cuerpo la grandeza
de un río bajo el misterio
de la luna llena.
El sortilegio de un fulgor
en un ritmo de copas
con luz de estrellas.
Un viaje sorprendido
hacia la esencia de la noche
que agita el tiempo.

Union Pacific Northwest
by Mike Owsley

Lyric, your name a song I hum on
the metra at night. Out of Ogilvie,
out of Park Ridge and Pingree Road
now out of time.

Your hand,
if it were here it would
be in mine. If only you had made
it to the station in time.
You would be mine too.

Now? Alone,
steel trees reach great heights.
Their roots are numerous and they
snake along beside the train.
In this analogy, are the
cars leaving Chicago nutrients,
which fuels a mighty metal forest?
Or rather are they solitary gods
builders of a brand new ecosystem:
Piranesian designers of their prisons,
where they confine themselves.

The roads turn to towns and
the towns to the country.
And the wind, a
whistling birdsong, lyricaless
in a silent night devoid of us.

Pajarito
por Walter Alexis Velásquez Mendoza

¡Ámame, pajarito lindo!
Que hay mariposas
Hermosas en mi garganta
Y que por eso te dedico
Está romantica prosa
Que necesitas
 Que la sonrisa de tu boca
Roce ese sentimiento que llevo dentro
Que me tiene ardiendo
Con ternura y sin sosiego
¡Ámame, pajarito lindo!

Shelf Life
by Mark Fleisher

This friendship
solid and strong
or so I thought
so I thought
he thought as well

This friendship
begins to fray
around the edges

This friendship
a misunderstanding
eats away at the heart

This friendship
misinterpretations
about who said
what to whom when

This friendship
beyond repair
beyond redemption
perhaps not if
time and space granted

This friendship
does it carry
an expiration date
unseen or ignored?

And so it is
And so it goes
This friendship

The Ancients
by Carmen Gray

Time passes
it is a path of fallen petals
strewn across soundlessly, like dew drops
upon fresh blades of grass
they are just as temporal
each petal holds a moment
whereby a day was lived,
gladly or sadly
depending on the circumstances
they disintegrate
softly curling inward
becoming part of the footpath
where little bare feet tread
scattering with the wind
and nestling into the ground
resting under layers
of newly fallen petals
the soil and rocks
collectively guarding all
the knowledge and secrets
of each day lived

The Cost
by Terry Allen

In a land whose business was business,
in railway yards or along sidings
in the early years when hours were long
and labor was hard in the rains of summer
and in the freezing winds and snows of winter

they were there at their posts
near moving trains, the switchmen
who sometimes suffered
from crushed bones and amputations,
some crippled for life.

Searching
by Trev Wainwright

Ben Thompson was his name, he of Wild West fame
Said to be good with a gun and at the poker game
Came from Yorkshire with his family at the age of eight
Settled in Austin in the Texas State
Later found he was able, to make living at the poker table
Fought in the Civil War and More
And then, in Abilene running a gambling den
In 1881 his career as a lawman in Austin begun
Doing well as it was said the crime Rate sharply fell
Of his adventures there were more
Till he was murdered in San Antonio in 1884
Buried in Oakwood Cemetery an' I've a mind his grave to find
Then I can, pay homage to a fellow Yorkshireman

Walls

by Carmen Calatayud

What I told you under the covers
is everything I believe.

The skeleton of a horse runs along the wall.

You must climb over walls to take your place.
Those in charge, if you wait for them
to do the right thing,
you'll be waiting 17 lifetimes.

Listen to the bones in a galloping horse.

Don't awaken to a day that has already
been written and pretend to hope.
The right thing won't come to you.
You have to take it.

Years fall off the calendar of a horse's frame.

There are walls everywhere.
Your job is to knock them down with your eyes.
Then go toward tenderness.

Horse is your ancestor.
Ancestors never disappear when you are conjuring a life.

What I told you under the covers
is everything I believe.

Atonement Three
by John Chinaka Onyeche

27th October is the raging sea,
the quaking earth...
still the eye looks ahead
beyond the quake
beyond the raging sea
where there is eternal stillness
in the lyrical whisper of peace
in the palm of God or fate
(just how do you discern God's voice?
and how do you answer it
when life merely splashes on you
and stains the frock of dream?)
if all life is a storehouse...
just how do you name its stocks?

My soul trudges, this cup is heavy on my lips
still I long to swill to the dreg
and listen to my slurp

Husband is Putting on Blues Records

"You have to make a decided effort to not get seduced by the Blues."
— Al Jarreau

by Adrian Ernesto Cepeda

For me
the blues are intense
and rich. He knows how
the effect from the first note,
so elegant and complex and
damned sexy. For me, it starts
before the chords open, the way
he slyly teases, as I watch him
slowly takes the wax record
out of the sleeves, his fingers
gently touch, holding up
the sides, his eyes trained,
focusing intensely as he blows
twice, watching the dust
rise from the vinyl, for me—
feels like his fingers softly
gliding over my skin, for me,
in the mood, already from
the first sound of the guitar
strings, blushing down south
moving closer hearing the voice
crackling, he loves taking my hand,
my husband reaches out to dance,
the only light the eyes between
our shadows, one color, blues
always reignites, for me, he knows—
my anticipation electric while he
spins the LP on the turntable,
truly loving the sound when
the needle hits our groove.

Thank You, Mireya Vela

We Used to Live on Icebergs
by Gerry Rodriguez

We were left, the inconvenient daughters
of fathers who didn't want us,
fathers who sacrificed their pregnant daughters,
fathers who sold the bodies of the daughters
who belonged to the earth,
fathers who covered the mouths of the daughters
they could not bring themselves to see.

We used to live on icebergs, running in place.
cursed to be dreamers until our feet sank,
submerging our bodies in the stagnant water
where thirsty mosquitoes lay
their eggs under our skin.

We floated, discarded, our faces lifted to the moon.
And the moon wept stars that fell
like diamonds, piercing the flesh of the earth,
and we rose, flames reaching for the sun
where we became ornaments
for men who gaze at stars.

We watched our fathers fall from their thrones,
their eyes poisoned by blue light,
their faces wrapped in cellophane.

We Do not Want your Privilege
by Rolando Serna

We do not want your privilege
Checking your privilege is not
Us wanting your privilege
If your privilege
is
won
by oppression
We do not wish to pay you in kind
Complicating issues by accusing the victims
Of not separating issues and
Creating the reason
They will not be
 heard
Seems kind of "white" of the court
Not wanting to set a precedent that would
Force the courts hand, in the future
To help other
Intersections of minorities
And then having the audacity to
Write it in the summary brief
Shows that the higher courts
Know nothing or care nothing
Of the minorities that have yet to
Be
identified
The 1851 cries of "Aren't I a Woman"
Will echo in the future
We are looking for the day that
The cry of am I not a human
Will no longer have to
Be, heard
 in order
To realize that humans
have only one enemy

The predator
that seeks to destroy humans
 are other humans
We do not want your privilege
We want equality
We do not wish to take from you
We do not like what
sustains you
To eliminate an oppressor
replace them with another
Will never serve
humans
It will only serve
the oppressor
The reason people with privilege
do not want to acknowledge it
The realization of the pain and suffrage
they cause
Might
 Not
 move them to change
It might move them
to cause more pain
To keep the oppressed
silent
Making them see that what the oppressed
had been accusing them of
Was not the truth
It was just a glimpse
Of what the monster
 inside them is capable of
We do not want your privilege
We only seek our rights
As humans no different
 than you
Having your privilege
might create
monsters out of us.

That Photo on the Wall
by Gerald Jatzek

The five of them
wore hats and coats.
Their instruments grew from their hands.

They played by ear. Their names were lost.
They were a band from Latvia. That's all

I know.

Their songs were full of grace and beauty.
Although I've never heard them play,

their music shields me every time
I hear the sound
of marching feet.

3.25.2022
by Julia-Paz

I want to be good enough.
Good enough for you and good enough for me. I want to feel like the sun.
Bright and burning.
And when you look directly at me,
I hope it hurts.
I want to be a constellation like you.
Made of wonders and stardust,
with people always looking up to me
searching for guidance.
I want to glow,
lighting up your world for just a second.
Almost as if I simply want you to take note of my absence, missing me
deeply.
Even if it is just for a moment.
I want to be the ocean.
Sending waves of my affection
to crash upon you before pulling it all back.
I want my smile to mean something real and nurturing. I want to give you a
piece of me
with the hope that you'll actually hold on to it. But I know you'll just throw
it away.
Because I am not enough.
I am not the sun or a constellation,
an ocean or a glow.
My smile is not guidance
and you want no part of me.

To Draw Water From A Barren Well
by Ashlynn Delias

I've got to dig deep, so I reach,
Into my soul, only to find a shadow,
The puddle of a pothole–more shallow,
Than the pocket of women's jeans,
You can barely squeeze, your fingertips past the seams of my soul.
I've got to dig deep, so I reach, only to find,
A poet's voice trafficked by, a stream of heart-break songs on repeat.
My voice has been stewing and steaming in a pot of pitiful feelings,
Redolent with heart felt angst,
But when you leave the pot on the stove too long it burns into flavorless
mutilation. I've got to dig deep, so I jam my decaying fingers into the gaping
hole of my chest, Only to strike gravel–the fertile soil of once powerful prose,
now cracked. And dried. And disfigured by– its own seeds that became
weeds, when the right person did wrong by them, I try to dig deep, and draw
poetry from my soul,
Yet unfailingly thump into hollow, hardened, and impenetrable bone.
Is that what the loss of love does?
Deceives you into believing that love comes, only in the tempting shape of
a rugged man, That love dwells only in the confines of caring hands, but
Love was there in the solace of the vacuum before the creation of humanity
began; Love thrums forcefully through native lands, In the river veins that
pulse through neglected soil, in the Chicana sun that blesses the white man's
toil, Love is the ancient, powerful wind that blows through the mesquite
panhandle of the Rio Grande–It's rustling through objectified, sun-burnt
brown Latina hair. Love. Was. There. Before it was capitalized into an
unattainable product reserved for a chosen few, who can mold their souls to
consumerist plans.
I dig deep into my soul, that vibrates blue beneath my chest,
To find the remnants of an innocent heart, before man only saw it as a
breast.

Ars Poetica
by Elisa A. Garza

> *"I poeti sono impossibili"*
> **— Alessandro Carrera**

Poets are impossible, you say,
the title of your book translated
in the faculty newsletter. That is all
I know of what you say about poets,
since I do not read Italian. Others say
poetry is dead, over, yesterday.

Not so. The poets are not dead.
We are forever today and always
tomorrow. A poem congeals
the was, is, could be, yet reveals
all that lies beyond and between.
Poems are more than the possible:

poets imagine all that is not.
What else but a poem could tell us
the story behind Hopper's diner,
or surmise what The Lady wrote,
wrote again in her letter while Vermeer
painted, painted her for months?

Poets are impossibly hopeful:
a poem feels, deeply, truly
sees the ocean in every tear,
hears the notes a voice may sing.
Impossibly poetic, how could a poet
believe, without metaphor or song?

MASKS

by Luisa Govela

It is not easy
To be alive
Surrounded by masks.
Other people have nervous,
Non-smiling eyes.
You fear the hand you don't shake,
The hug you don't give,
The smile you don't share.
In the park, you fail to recognize
Your next-door neighbor,
Hidden behind a mask.
As in a divorce,
The virus lays claim
To half of everything:
Half a face,
Half a home,
Half of friends and kin.
And, if you are lucky,
Perhaps half a job.

IT COULD HAPPEN AGAIN
by Sandra Dolores Gómez Amador

It could happen again! It is not something uncommon. The paperwork on
the Sargent's desk indicates 1294 cases of justifiable homicide.

Half of them were Hispanic inmates
who never really knew how to speak.

Because that's the issue with not being born with a bald eagle inside your tongue:
your voice won't be heard
even if you beg, if you implore,
if you crawl across the floor.

It could happen again! No one will look
for an immigrant's corpse. No one will ask. They all look the same. It could
happen again.

It will happen again.

Ghosts

by Michael Gerleman

How sad to be a ghost.
half in one world, half in another,
to carry so much wisdom, so much experience,
and no way to communicate,
but through children's games at slumber parties,
Ouija boards in college dorms,
Psychics in carnivals,
and old women staring into teacups.

We don't respect the wisdom of the dead.
They are consigned to glimpses
in the corners of our eyes,
momentary reflections in windows,
and their voices sound like moonlight sliding on glass.

Antonio Orendain, ¡Presente!
by Nephtalí De León

one more giant passes by
through the corridor of mystery
and the corridor of time,
a man so robust and so fine,
el líder campesino
Antonio Orendain…

miles and miles he walked by
in La Casita, Texas,
where I went to school
furrows after furrows,
miles and miles of surcos
worked by honest
tired hands…

he faced governors
and challenged presidents
in Washington .D.C.
líder of the farmworkers
of Texas, giant state,
where things still grow...
God's gift to humankind ...

I marched with Orendain
and Jesús Moya
in Muleshoe, Texas,
I read my poetry with Tony
on the steps of the Capitol
in Austin, Texas

I walked with Giants
humble, strong farmworkers
and rested in the shadow
of the greatest, dressed in black,

always with bandana underneath
a matching with-his-clothes
black hat, Antonio Orendain,
who just soared like an eagle
straight to Tata Tonatiuh, the Sun!

this giant of a man
is now our spirit guide
forever present in our myth and lore
Antonio Orendain, presente !

Sometimes
by Enedina Irene

Sometimes I just know-
I know-
that I don't deserve it.

Even though I know I do.

They are true blue magic-
wrapped in perfection-
powdered with chaos-
that makes my heart leap.

I grow a little more, every time, every day-
when they smile at me-
and speak to me-
and tell me all about the things that live within the gray.

Never, do we not cherish the moments.
Especially the pain.

The pain is what guides us-
It's a keeper of time-
a reminder-
a challenge-
that they and I-
always survive.

And that is why sometimes I just know-
I know-
that I don't deserve it.

Because I've earned it.

The sorrow that lingers-
the love that thrives-

the forever lust that seethes in the divine.

I know that I've earned it-
though I may not deserve it.

BESIDE BROKEN CLOUDS
by Uchechukwu Onyedikam

Besides our hands clasped in
devotion at the face of misfortune
counting on the wand of God
to sway a sign in the room…
thus to record another will
for the New Testament's solace
Beside yesterday, beside broken clouds
I sunk back clutching my body with
the discipline of the whip, closing
my eyes as life goes blurred —

The world is ending up with you
next to me this comely dayspring
after we've had some coloured
moment of notes last night — all
written in a little short story of how
much time crawls slowly away…
leaving us handcuffed to this harassing
thought of a jailbird flapping its wings
yet wouldn't catch flight

As it has given, we are left to ourselves
to wonder and then let our inflated joy
wash itself into oblivion as we sit on
the edge of this river watching its flow
seizing everything we ever had —
including the still-body of our 3yo son —
because the underbelly of this river
has many things it feeds on. Like —
our wedding bells ringing through the
creeping darkness yet with tenderness
of our boy as the lightning with fire

The Gathering of Faithfuls

After Rasaq Malik Gbolahan

by Mohammed U. Yusuf

The sun recedes behind the clouds
as faithfuls flock their temples

to soothe the anguish of taste.
The muezzins ascend the minarets,

proclaiming the adhān: birds
chirp the refrains of their calls

while they journey back to nestle.
Raising cupped palms skywards,

they beseech the Almighty.
They lower them soberly with faith

hoping their fervent requests would
return in a manifold of blessings.

Vaults of autumn
by Joselin Mejía Garcia, Mexico

Diverse are the lines of life
in the year that in splendor is consuming.
In the dark forest the wasteland
swaps in the creek's kiss.

Thus man finds himself
In autumn, like an opening question.
Is a man young, old or eternally brand-new?
This the spirit will unveil.

The past sprouts in flowers,
field flooding, bridge of words.
Where the pier breaks,
I stand
as an adolescent, as an adult,
showing my son
the way.

Throwing pebbles into the river
so that him does not have to inherit them,
teaching him to sit in the clear waters
of silence.

Let's embrace the years,
let's love the morning light,
let's breathe in the unfathomable night.

Let beauty and love go
when it is a withered skin,
once in a while wash off
so many eternities.

The leaves of grass will become litter,
but will keep their charm.
It is the tree of life, my son, a prodigy
and in each leaf, a mystery.

The Boxer
by G.G. (Giana Gallardo) Hesterberg

The boxer
enters the ring,
feet light as feathers,
swift as a fox,
eyes green with grit,
bright as the hills
in Georgia.

Left foot forward,
left hand to protect,
bounce-step, cross,
left hook,
bob and weave,
Bounce and leave.

Lace up for the
next match,
back against the ropes,
southpaw stroke
knocks him down,
face on the ground,
slowly, he gets up.

Running
on the sunny side
of homemade eggs
and neighborhood
streets
Pop never missed a fight
Shadowboxing
the little boy within.

Gloves up
in the steel
fortress.

Sirens call,
unable
to penetrate
his walls.

Lambrusco,
Don Peligro,
and Jesus
keep him warm.

He looks out,
sees four little girls,
smiles,
and chases the dawn.

For my Pop

In Ixtli In Yolotl: Hay Cosas que Nunca se te Darán de Vuelta
by Joann González

rostro de mujer
rostro indígena
rostro que viste de injusticia

cuáles ojos lloran por el pueblo
enséñale que es tener una voz
a ese rostro dile que sí

ve lo, cómo busca la oportunidad
con una fortaleza infinita
a ese rostro ponle atención

rostro que es ignorado
rostro digno de libertad y respeto
rostro lleno de amor

In Ixtli In Yolotl: There are Things that Will Never be Given Back to You

face of a woman
an indigenous face
a face who wears injustice

whose eyes cry out for their village
teach them what it means to have a voice
say yes, to that face

look at it, how it searches for an opportunity
with infinite fortitude
pay attention, to that face

a face which is ignored
a face worthy of liberty and respect
a face full of love

Esperanza Is Another Name for Hope
by Jean Hackett

As we waited to vote,
our minds wandered from ballot issues,
distrust, division, and spite
to marvel at pollinator gardens along gravel trails
winding towards the precinct doors.

We crowded around the fuzzy sumptuousness
of Gregg's blue mist to share in the collective magic
as hundreds of orange butterflies clustered,
five, six, or more, to a single flower.

Monarchs? A young woman holding her elderly mother's arm wondered.
A few larger, striped ones, a man with crinkled eyes replied.
Mostly queens this time of year.
And everyone picked up their ears to listen
as he described varieties of butterflies and host plants,
and nodded in understanding
when he explained the importance of native species.

The line inched forward, then stalled.
We exchanged smiles, some infused with desire
to create more pollinator gardens,
as configurations of golden sulphurs
danced about arrays of low-slung white mist
and bushes of sunny esperanza,
which translates into hope.

I Majored in Writing and Now I am a Copywriter
by Paula Andrea Córdova García

I went to school for Writing for 4 years
I wrote hundreds of essays, read thousands of pages on literary theory
only to end up working in marketing.
I don't complain because I still make a living off writing
even if all I write are short phrases
that try to convince people to buy ____ (the product I am currently working for)
and the phrases are so short, so short
but they take so much, so much of my time that by the end of the day I'm left
with nothing to write.
I went to school for Writing for 4 years and I ran out of letters
I don't have any time for reading but I must pay rent
I must pay for the place where I live and for everything else
and I tell you "I went to school for Writing for 4 years and I feel
like I don't know how to write anymore"
I am sick of typing about dresses, shoes, and furniture that don't belong to me
but still, I get paid for working as a copywriter and that pays my rent
so I can whisper *I love you* in your ear,
so I can smell your skin,
so I can say that this bed where we fuck, I paid for with my writing
I build this space so I can say "this home is also yours"
and I sweep, and I mop, and I fold clothes
—you know how much I hate folding clothes—
so these few square feet in Mexico City can belong to me at least for the rest of the month
and I keep working as a copywriter,
15 words and clicking, clicking, clicking,
so at the end of the day we can watch one of those movies we don't understand
in some streaming service we can't afford
but that doesn't matter because we are going to kiss for 2 hours straight
instead in this room that costs the modest amount of 500 thousand
characters per month

Drop of Time
by Michael Owens

Michael! listen to me,
Don't do that now
We will be late!

Yours the background voice
When I was recording the greeting
On our home answering machine.

Now friends tell me they
Love to call and listen
Because it is so us.

I listen every day to your voice
Frozen in that drop in time
Among forty years of marriage.

I can recall every moment that day
We were on our way to Church
With the kids, grandkids and friends.

Everything happened so fast
You turned in the doorway
Looked at me, eyes wide open
Slipped and hit your head

The fall left you helpless
Then within a week.
Gone.

Leaving me here
With only your recorded voice
And a love I feel everywhere.

Dine in
by Spartakos Anagnostaras

Don't wait for me.
It's an early night tonight.
I stand like a statue.
The night and your lips blessed me
with years.
I want to find flowers.
I want to tell you
Cheers.
I want
to find roses
in cold hearts.
Empty streets.
I want to unlock
the morning with the cats.
Cloudy sky.
Who can envy the morning
when no solutions come?
It's a cold morning.
I need solutions
for next week
and life is your forgotten
lighter on the table.

Jenny in the Bottle
by Laura Peña

She wears flowy, flower pants,
She flashes her infectious smile,
That high piercing laugh of delight
You know when she's near
The room tilts and we twirl with
Her on the beach as she proclaims,
"Thrust those hips, ladies!"
"Our soft, animal bodies need release!"
Tequila shots and
Walking to a town called Mars,
We'll follow you anywhere, Jenny girl
You choose when you want
To go back into the bottle
And you don't wait for anyone
To let you out

Driving Next to the Llano River in Marble Falls, Texas
by Shannon Hardwick

Muddy boots wade against
the window closing
tight the spine your
hands reaching
for a glass of milk
for the child not
in her room she's
dotted her way past
the field buried heavy
with rain maybe that's
how her legs stuck together
in the waiting it happens—
one day you're in your own
mother's car she's
crying then a bell rings
in the distance now you're
the one driving trying not to
spill a glass of milk &
holding it up to the noon
light think maybe you shouldn't
dig up her boots with a knife.

Walk With My Dead Tía Abuela At the Neighborhood Festival
by Violeta Garza

The mood--
mariachis vibrating,
pink concha earrings sparkling,
limpias for donation.

It's 100 degrees under tree branches.

My tía abuela and I
finesse our farmer's
tans.

Mid-trumpet,
a rebellious mariposa
confides that I should revel
    more. My teenage, middle-aged, and viejita selves balk at the notion of joy.

           We don't know how to deserve better.

        Smudge smoke and love advice
           trickle up the rooftop while I pretend I'm not
       looking for my mother's spirit.

Aftermath

by John C. Mannone

The white-noise rain
amplifies the memory
of nightmares. The splash
of blood drenching down
with the clash of muskets
        and bayonet steel.
The deafening storm
of cannons, clouds
of smoke after the flash
of powder, the final clap
of thunder, and applause.
        I awaken,
everything is soaking wet
and green. I'm on my belly,
the ceiling fans chopping air
morph into Hueys. The wall-
paper curls under the heat
of napalm. Beads of sweat
glimmer in the orange glow
through the window, open,
not a breeze.
        I struggle
to stand, work my way
to the sill. I see nothing,
nothing but the expanse
of desert, nothing
        but rubble,
        no one.

The burden tossed between tousled sheets
by Victoria Lopez

The burden tossed between tousled sheets;
In the direction of what is hoped for
Against that which cannot be seen.
When shall sleep come?
To steer toward a future
Today, my knees buckle.
To dream of mornings
Spent alongside comfort,
When day does not break until the evening.
The hour passed, the day has gone by,
The year has come again, and I,
Captured in an eye
Which sees all that I am —
My head is bowed once more.
When shall sleep come?

Nuestra Vida
by Vito del Valle

Ghosts of the barrio haunt the streets at night
Cruising in ethereal lowriders
Gunshot wounds still visible through their Dickies
Oldies thump on the radio
Tattooed, feathered, Aztec warrior in an Impala
With his chola beside him
A black jaguar in the backseat
Skeleton mariachis beneath a streetlight
    singing Amargos Tragos
These are the dead
This is our past
    ancient and modern
Forever in our memories
    and imprinted in our cut out hearts
Let us sing together, hermano
Let us drink together
Let us dance together
Porque
    nuestra raza es
    nuestra vida

My Lovely Valley
by Yelitza Tibisai Saenz

Without much thought,
There are many unforgettable memories.
They require much taste,
But in the end, they will never be erasable.

From weekends at the lake,
To fish at South Padre Island.
I have come to realize that I'm not wealthy or arrogant,
I have the freedom to fly.

Since my youth I have known about my Mexican roots,
I always knew my Spanish was going to help me
somehow.
What I didn't know was that I would be judged for
being Mexican American,
I was left without the desire to talk.

I never thought I would write in Spanish.
It was just a stigma with negativity tied.
My native tongue is unique, but I often make it vanish
But somehow, I manage to hide my pride.

Here, we are all the same.
We all like tacos and chitterlings
Everyone knows we are all particular
But because of the tacos we're not slim and we all have
family in Tamaulipas.

My lovely valley, I will never forget you.
You will always be in my heart, like a memorial tattoo.

Mi Valle Querida
by Yelitza Tibisai Saenz

Sin pensar mucho,
Hay experiencias inolvidables.
Requieren muchísimo gusto,
Pero al final siempre serán imborrables.

From weekends at the presa,
To fishing at SPI.
I have come to realize that I'm no fresa,
I have the freedom to fly.

Desde joven yo sabía que tenía raíces mexicanas,
Siempre supe que mi español me iba ayudar.
Lo que no sabía era que me juzgaban por ser Mexicana Americana
Ni ganas me daban de hablar.

I never thought I would write in Spanish.
It was just a stigma with negativity tied.
My native tongue is unique, but I often make it vanish
But somehow, I managed to hide my pride.

Aquí todos somos iguales.
A todos les gustan los tacos y tripas
Todos saben que somos individuales
Pero por los tacos no somos flacos y tenemos gente en Tamaulipas.

Mi valle querida, I will never forget you.
Siempre estarás en mi corazón, like a memorial tattoo.

DIVIDED
by Érika Elisa Garza

I salute two flags
I think in Spanish most of the time
Excepto the numbers que son tercos
And they want to be American.
I am a proud Mexican
Who has lived most of her life
In the U. S.
I feel divided, torn apart,
My heart doesn't know
Any more what or how to feel.
I will never forget my raíces
Ni mi lenguaje
Pero a ti, United States,
He empezado a quererte
Aunque comencé odiándote.
I know it is hard to understand
This feeling, cuando el orgullo
For my birth country is so big.
I live in this border
Across the river that kills so many
Across the wall that tries to stop newcomers,
Justice is not always really fair.
I see memories, I feel my confusion
In both languages.
I am half and half.
I cannot deny I am not the same as I was.
United States, I salute your flag,
México, do not be jealous,
For I loved you first.

An Egyptian folk tale
by Shaswata Gangopadhyay (INDIA)

Don't throw stones at a fellow who truly loves you
those stones'll come back to you someday or other

It is an Egyptian folk tale, the written version in the proverb
but you didn't obey it, rather as a first lover
you ditched him, leaving him alone
putting chewing gum casually in your mouth
at 8 o'clock past 10 in the morning,
you are crossing the quiet desert,
no mirage is visible, only broken skeletons
of camels lie scattered here and there
sometimes after the sun will look like a ruthless hammer
after pulling out from your rucksack the last bottle of soft drinks
you being exhausted, will roll on the ground senseless
sense when regained, you listen to the wind of the storm :
It's the curse of the God of sands and deserts :

Throughout your life you all alone will go on searching water
you will earn money, enjoy solvency, but never you will get a beloved

Building Blocks
by Alan Cherian Puthenpurayil

Life is the game of building blocks!
However hard we try,
One block will remain missing.

That missing block is in everything and
In everyone's life.
Read Chaucer's Canterbury,
See the curves of Eiffel,
And explore the life of Nick Vujicic.

Nothing is perfect,
These are not the weaknesses
But, rather the hallmarks of the wonderful creations.

I Tried to Give You my Star
by Gustavo Barahona-López

You said if I ever made a star
you'd nurture it's light.
You said it was all
you ever wanted.
You said make it so.

So when I plucked a star
from inside my throat
and called it rosemary.
Forgive me for wanting
to share its overwhelming
radiance with you.

Forgive that my little star
was still covered in my blood,
which is to say your blood.
Forgive that I expected you
to give it your devotion.

You see, from the moment
I plucked the star
out of my body, I knew
I had been given a new life.

I had to become a sun to teach
my star how to be incandescent.
You, however, could not look
into the brightness for long.

You must know how much I wanted
to bring you into the light.
You must know I can no longer
stand with you in the dark.

Phoenix
by Jasmin Garcia

Like the phoenix
I rise from my cremated flesh
From the ashes of my former self
And the wisdom I once knew
I soar with featherless wings as
Embers glaze like honey and drip from
My new self.
Nothing? I am nothing?
I am everything you can only dream of.
I am the dream, the REM, the breaths
That depart your lips
Your heart pumps pulps perfectly synchronized
To the sound of my cries
Your sweat drips from cheek to neck
My heat is nothing? Nothing?
I can burn anything. Everything.

Engulfed within the flames of resilience,
I rejoice in a renewed existence.

I always knew you were a portrait
by Mark Esperanza

I always knew you were a portrait
A showcase in McNay
Brush strokes to wave your black hair
Black waves over a soft shoulder
Should I ever come across your smile
I'll dare to worship your lips
Slip a kiss to a glass frame
Forever from your sweet embrace

I always knew you were photography
A sepia tone classic
The lights bending to capture secrets
Capture moments hidden in your eyes
I beg to uncover the moon
Move stars to align us together
To get a snapshot of us in a constellation
A captured fish, a stinging scorpion

I always knew you were timeless
A fragile stone in an ancient museum
Belonging to life cursed by time
I'm always time traveling
Grappling with caressing your soul
So I may bring my heart to order
Or respect your wish to be friends
An end to all we're feeling

I always knew you'd become poetry
Romance this strong belongs to literature
Your voice an everlasting sound
A lyrical song with a Houston twang
Your written words, sugar sweet
Sleeping lullaby to my dreams

And I dream a name I cannot speak
My adored rose, lovely enchanting you

My adored rose, lovely enchanting you

Magic
by Gabriella Gutiérrez y Muhs

When the sorcerers in you awake
tell them it's midnight,
they might remain asleep

you might remain believing

When the magicians in you decide
it's time to cook the meal
of forgetfulness
help chop the chiles of memory
time for tomatoes, potatoes, avocados, distress,
to return home threaded by mint
when they descent consume them, the words
until you know where to lie, where to sit, where to
belong,
where to remain, where to gaze

When the goddess of words descends
from your heavenly harem of food, rejoice

just know the crackers, the melon, the figs of
restitution abound
in the fields of your creativity.

when they descend.

THE BAMBOO GROVE BENT DOWN
by Guna Moran

The bent bamboo
Was just a shoot once upon

It cannot say the same
To its offshoot
Straightening its waist

Father looks at the material earth
Son towards the sky

Never looks eye to eye

The skyward shoots keeps gazing
At the shining stars
They are short of time for the father
Caught in the whirlwind of daily chores

The wind does not only spin the bamboo shrub at the
spot
It also severs the head of the shoots

After a long time
The necklace shoots too turn into shrub

Bereft of the tip
It becomes useless
Only then
If the shoots come to senses
Time does not allow time

A Letter to my Baby's Twin Myoma
by Denise Melanie Du Lagrosa

I felt a bump on my belly. I thought I was just getting fat
I pressed, I pushed, I squeezed. "Shape up!" my father would tease.
It was the first quarter of the year. My monthly visitor was long overdue
I pressed, I pushed, I squeezed. Life inside of me felt anew.
It was summer near the full moon that the fat we thought we knew
My doctor pressed, pushed, and squeezed the twin myoma of my baby beau
She couldn't hear a heartbeat. She was in disbelief.
My belly, she pressed, pushed, and squeezed. I sobbed on my handkerchief.
Myoma is as big as my baby's head. Few others size of 5 cents
My baby pressed, pushed, and squeezed for space as well as nutrients
I was preparing for a normal delivery. I even practiced my breathing
That when my doula pressed pushed and squeezed, my baby would go out in a breeze.
But then one day I stood from the sofa bed. A patch of water on my dress colored red.
My belly didn't feel pressed pushed and squeezed.
My baby couldn't wait to go out instead
And so we rode a cab to the hospital. I called my doctor, my mother, and my HR.
I said it's time to press, push and squeeze. I was so afraid I may rest in peace.
My delivery needs to be a C section and my doctor wanted to have a glimpse
Of my myoma that pressed pushed and squeezed. But they couldn't see it.
It was on eclipse.
And when I first heard my baby cry, she was wrapped in a purple swaddle to dry.
I wanted to hold her press push and squeeze. She was taken to the NICU
and I couldn't breathe
Now my baby sleeps peacefully amidst the storm. She coos, sneezes, and squeals
As I wrap her in my arms, press, push and squeeze, she sleeps on my chest
like a princess and a pea.

Lodestar
by PW Covington (New Mexico, USA)

I came into this world
Reserved
Intending to do no thing
To walk in all directions
Everywhere at once
Eyes open
To keep my own gait and pace
Tenderly
Lingering where I should want in the moment
For the day, the year, or longer

I came into this city
Marching
One of legion
Eyes flying, quick to the flame
Where no soft-soled feet could follow
Lightening-passion cocaine sex and trauma
Never quenched

Mountain meadows are not mirages
Reflecting winter whiteglow snow-shine gleam
That light is true as stone, and death and love
And the ocean floor, vaulted to the sky
As tiny and viscous centuries churn past
Snows fall and melt
The mountains do not notice

I plan to leave this world untidily
My best words yet unpublished
My best loves flashing red like a beacon
Lodestar true
       and ever shifting

Bendición
by Yari "Porta Rock" Pares

The request asked by many,
Taught to us by our
Elders and passed on from parent
To child letting us know that
Everything will be okay
Bendición,
Always being reminded to
Ask for it
Or else
Be casted into eternal damnation
As told to you by the powers that
be whom
In many cases was "mami", who after you were scolded usually
Had nothing more to say
Bendición
Don't ever attempt
To enter or leave the house
Without asking for it
Or else there would be
Hell to pay!
Bendición
Always wondered
If the friends
That I have lost along
The way
Forgot to request
it
before saying
goodbye on their last
day
Bendición
Grateful to hear
Dios Te Bendiga ,which means "God Bless You In Spanish"

Even if things
Don't seem to be going
The right way
Bendición
I even got my kids
Requesting it from me
Now a days
Bendición
Que Dios Te bendiga

Who's That Girl?
by Diosa Xochiquetzalcóatl

¿Que quién soy y adonde voy?
I am Citlali, a speckle that sparkles under the sun.

But, where are you from?
Soy del mundo de las estrellas, del mucho más allá.
Adriana la Xicana - de la galaxia Andrómeda.

¿Y por qué vivo en una bóveda?
Soy hija de la luna, hija del Mictlan,
hija del inframundo y las cavernas de Teotihuacan.
Soy una itzcuintli de Xolotl.

¿Entonces, cuál es tu complot?
Recordar. Recordar. Recordar.

Yo vine a este mundo a recopilar.
My life from Atl'antix, purple mountains, and Tulúm
My life as love-making Diosa and as tochtli on the
moon.
My time as sacerdotisa; my time as slave.
My time as caballero, my time as knave.

I am...
commander-in-chief of a nave big and wide
with my trusted copiloto, Cutie-Q, by my side.

Yo soy...
guardiana de calavera - Hun-Tijax is her sacred name.
A rainbow obsidian crystal skull camina conmigo as I
regain...

Memoria. Memoria. Memoria.
¿Quién soy?¿A donde voy? ¿Cuál es mi triste historia?

¿Triste mi historia? ¡Nada de eso!
Aunque no me han regalado ni siquiera un solo hueso.

¿A qué viene todo esto?
Trasmutar. Trasmutar. Trasmutar.

Yo vine a este mundo a sanar
el ataque a mi chakra vocal,
y los traumas que giran en el gran espiral.

¿A qué viniste sagrada nahual?
Amar. Amar. Amar. Amar.

The physical matter does not matter.
Geography is just a place.
Who I am and where I'm from
is just a 3D chase.
Solo se que vine a aprender
how to love this human race.

Who's that girl? Es la pregunta that many want to
know.
Not just where I came from, but where I want to go.
Only this, I know...

Soy, doy, vengo y voy....
Un recuerdo. Una memoria. Una recopilación.
Un misterio. Una historia. Una fuerte trasmutación.
Desenvoltura. Desentierro. Una gran revolución.
Convocatoria. Gran silencio. Sagrada sanación.

Ella es...
Nosotros somos...
Amor. Amor. Amor.

Hoy llevo el altar en mi boca
por Diosa Xochiquetzalcóatl

Al decirle tu nombre al viento,
de mi boca brotan flores de cempohualxochitl.
El fuego de tu memoria
enciende la llama de mi corazón de concreto.
Las gotas de mi saliva
seducen a la nubes, dejándolas impregnadas con rastros
de tu rostro.
Y cada vez que Tlaloc derrama sus lágrimas
de mi boca florece un jardín de oro que siempre susurra
tu nombre.

love/death
by Karen Cline-Tardiff

do not disgrace language
by speaking against the power of my love

do not contest the truth of your eyes:
my love turns stone into bleeding

petal blushing under my touch
white to pink unto death

I invite you into my bedroom
plunge a stake in your mouth

will not let lies flow from
your mouth like water upon rocks

you can no more deny me
than you can rage against me

you call me hate, wicked, rot,
you don't understand my love

it is oxygen leaving your lungs
after you have died just a little

it is the whistle of a far train
in the dark of sleepless night

it is soil dropped onto the top
of a casket six feet in the ground

Prayer for Milk Weed
by Karen Cline-Tardiff

We spent the first summer of Covid
clearing our yard of all the milkweed.
It took hold of our little acre and threatened
to choke out all of beans and tomatoes,
peppers and squash, even the basil was
holding onto the barest square inch of dirt.
Sandy loam is what they call our soil.
It is a breeding ground for all the milk weed.
We would curse and pull until the root
came out whole, trying to stave off
the unrelenting march into the driveway.

Common milkweed grows quickly to two to four feet in height. It has a narrow vertical growth habit and thick, long, oblong green leaves that grow to about eight inches. Once established, milkweed spreads rapidly by self-seeding if seed pods are not removed.

The second summer of Covid we gave
up on gardening and let the milkweed
take over the tiny plot, braiding itself
through the wire meant to keep out deer
We would drive by on our way to
official store hours, fully masked,
and see butterflies flitting across our path.
On the way home with carefully sanitized
beans and tomatoes, peppers and squash,
we would see different butterflies and
bees skipping from flower to flower,
resplendent in their attention to the
milkweed which had been given free reign.

Common milkweed (Asclepias syriaca) is a native herbaceous perennial that appeals to butterflies—especially the monarch butterfly. Asclepias is the only plant family that serves as the host plant for monarch butterfly egg laying. The monarch larvae, the hatchling caterpillars, feed exclusively on milkweed leaves. Without milkweed, there can be no monarch butterflies.

Last year we sold the house, but I
took a minute to tell the new owners
about the butterflies they would be
tending, the bees striving to spread pollen
from milkweed to milkweed, and how
it was just best to let it run wild up to the driveway.
I told them to make sure it didn't steal
too close to the persimmon I had nursed
back from near death in a freak freeze.

Plants in the milkweed family are the single most important source of food for the threatened monarch butterfly, and planting a patch or two in your landscape is an important contribution to the continued existence of the species.

Once the snow clears and spring pops through the
cool hibernating grass, I will drive by the old house,
look down the driveway which used to be ours,
and I'll pray for butterflies and bees. And milkweed.

The usual suspects are attracted to common milkweed, including milkweed bugs (which don't do too much harm, in fact), aphids, whiteflies, scale insects, spider mites, thrips, and leaf miners. Use a hose, spray from a bottle, or fingernails to scrape off the offenders. Snails and slugs also love young tender milkweed plants. Snail bait works well and won't harm monarchs, but as the plants grow, the snail problem minimizes.

(words in italics are from "How to Grow and Care for Common
Milkweed" by David Beaulieu for The Spruce.)

Los sauces
por J. Villarreal

Los sauces se mecen en la rivera
se adentran en las orillas a brazos abiertos
se murmuran de vez en cuando.

Una suave armonía renace en la brisa.
     Mientras la serpiente duerme
     los pateros se abren paso a la deriva.
        Desprenden sombras de los carrizales

Una nube de gorrioncillos horada la noche obsidiana
     se cuela a campos floridos del norte.

Halcones en camuflage bajo mezquites
se abalanzan sobre ellos a los primeros gestos de luz.

Presas del miedo solo un puñado irrumpe el acecho
plumas desgarradas visten las nopaleras.

El día sangra más allá del amanecer
 las alas blancas susurran un sufrido arrullo.

Ante el peligro se estremecen los sauces
se escurre el río por las laderas
     y disparado el viento allana la rivera.

Los gavilanes se mecen en las aguas claras del cielo.

El aullido de los coyotes quebranta el inerme silencio.

Todos esperan…esperan…esperan…un nuevo amanecer

The willows
por J. Villarreal

The willows sway along the river
        step into shallows with open arms
                and whisper from time to time.

A measured humming hover in the breeze
        while *pateros* drift across the sleeping serpent
                pushing hidden shadows off the *carrizales.*

A flock of house sparrows pierces the obsidian night
        chasing feeding fields on the other side.

Camouflaged harriers perched on *mezquites*
        pounce on them between first strands of light.

Tangled in fear a handful scuffle away,
        feathers flutter on the spines of *nopaleras.*

The day bleeds beyond the sunrise
        and *alas blancas* echo a mourning song.

Startled the willows shudder
        the river scurries downstream
                the wind scrambles away.

Peregrines drift the free-flowing skies.
        Coyotes crack the stone-cold silence.

All wait…wait…wait …
for another day.

II.

From Our Editors

In All the Days Like Today
by Linda Romero

Days like today it's harder to get past being yelled at
than understand why I matter instead

Days like today I go back in my mind to what's wrong about me
and not what God has made of me instead

Days like today I'm forced to hold back tears
because I'm supposed to meet expectations instead

Days like today I can't even journal what's wrong
because it would be too illegible to make sense

Days like today it's easy to notice the pain in getting there
instead of being blessed by making it there to begin with

But in all of the days like today,
I remember those who stayed

In all the days like today
I remember where I started

In all the days like today
I know I did my best anyway

In all the days like today
I still have my words

And in all the days like today
I remember He gives me strength

I Never Knew Grief Until You Were Gone
by Linda Romero

I never knew grief until you were gone
Or what mourning really meant
We wouldn't know how quickly you would leave
And all the years I spent trying to mentally prepare myself
With cancer, or the three bouts of pneumonia
With a brain tumor that stole the man I recognized
I thought I would know what it would feel like
Except it was more gut wrenching
Silent then explosive
Depending on the day
Or the song
Or I could be crying in the shower
With nothing but anxiety and fear
And it still hurts
And pieces of me are forever gone
Grief replaced what you occupied
But now takes up less space
Maybe because I'm trying to remember
Memories instead how you left
Stories instead of tears
All the love
And the hope
That I'm trying to put into words

Hay días
por Eduardo Villarreal de los Reyes

1

Hay días que por más que salga el sol no amanece
y se quedan suspendidas las horas
en las madrugadas de los ojos y
el desasosiego es un gato que maulla rozando
la esperanza que traes a la altura de los tobillos.
Esos días no amanece
aunque termines un rosario, vayas a misa
o le reces a tu santo.
Vives un vía crucis,
 haces de ese día tu Viernes de Dolores
y como en el camino te has vuelto casi ateo,
ya no crees ni en reencarnación ni en resurrección
ni en las mujeres que no se enojan
o en las que dicen "en nada"
cuando les preguntas en qué piensan.

También hay días en que por más que cierras los ojos
no anochece.

Péndulo
por Eduardo Villarreal de los Reyes

2

Cuando el péndulo de la vida no avanza más,
agujas del recuerdo abrazan por un segundo
el misterio eterno.
Ya no hay tristeza, decreto o salmo.
Se borran las cicatrices del alma
ante el nuevo sueño total.
Se va de camino a Mictlán.

Gravedad
por Eduardo Villarreal de los Reyes

3

Largo y bello relámpago que al final
tuvo su dolor de trueno.
Tu pasado inmediato es un abismo de palabras
que no sucedieron.
Me quedo aquí obligado por la gravedad.
No hubo fuerza humana ni divina para separar
sus corazones.
Monasterio de rezos. El enigma del estigma.
Solamente queda la sombra del aire
paseándose por los muertos.

River
by Edward Vidaurre

all the **women**
in my home

were bronze.
their skin
like **river** stones

out of water

slippery
Moon milk
Stars

Women.

Milk moon   **stars**
slippery

water out of
Stones, river like

their skin
bronze, were
home

all the women in my home were

Moon

River

Stars

I HAVEN'T BEEN TO CHURCH
by Edward Vidaurre

since before the pandemic,
maybe even longer than that

I'm wearing my best, not a suit
my best, the brown shoes with laces

the button up shirt with a collar
& slacks with the shirt tucked in

the agua bendita once held by the gilt
is no longer available for my guilt

every bowl entering the Church
is dry, the bowl, as if aching

cracking, i swipe my fingers &
get nothing but dust and scratches

late as always, sliding across the back
wall looking for a place to sit

the looming eyes of St. Francis holding
a lamb, over my shoulder as I listen to

the congregation read from the screen,
"The Lord is my shepherd, I shall not want..."

I look around the pews & see the millionaires
saying it the loudest, we all want, we all want something
i think to myself, we all need something

& we sing, nevermind off-key, but sing our lies

the Church had a remodel, therefore a second
collection, I look at St. Francis and ask him for a dime

I could swear he smiled & the lamb bleated

III.

Youth Poems

Sola

Por fin puedo estar sola
Por fin puedo hacer lo que quiero
Pero por qué me siento tan triste y con ansiedad.
Por qué no estoy feliz
Por qué espero tu llamada
A la misma hora.
Será porque extraño tus consejos
o serán tus regaños.
o porque odio el silencio de esta casa.
Trato de distraerme de esta triste realidad
Pero lamentablemente no puedo.
Ahora espero meses para tu regreso
Pero por fin estoy sola.

YADIRA MEJÍA es alumna de décimo grado y actualmente asiste a la escuela preparatoria La Joya Early College. A Yadira en su tiempo libre le gusta leer. Le gusta escribir sobre su vida.

Viviendo en soledad

Con la mente y el corazón vacíos
Vagando por los pasillos de este edificio
Nada que ver, nada que esperar
Solo una pila de papeles que terminar

Sonrisas por aquí y por allá
Sabiendo que ninguna se dirige a él
Nada que ver, nada que esperar
Solo un ser más que hay que ignorar

¿Podría ser que es invisible?
Pues nadie lo toma en cuenta
Nadie sabe quién es
Ni como se encuentra

¿Qué valor tiene su vida?
Mas nadie la valora
Vive día tras día
Buscando compañía

No puede ser, no puede ser
Se aproxima alguien
¿Qué dice? ¿Qué hace?
Supo reconocer que no venían hacia él

Vean alrededor
Busquen almas perdidas entre la sociedad
Que en cada rincón hay alguien
Viviendo en soledad

ALEF HERNÁNDEZ es alumno de décimo grado y actualmente asiste a la preparatoria La Joya Early College. A Alef Hernández en su tiempo libre le gusta pintar, dibujar y tocar el piano. Le gusta escribir sobre la vida en general y las cosas que pasan por su mente.

Life in a shell

Dark fills my world
There is no lights around
Filled with a empty void
Don't know where I am
Don't know how I am
I'm just filling a empty shell
Hiding behind a mask
No one knowing who I am
Hiding everything

La vida en un caparazón

La oscuridad llena mi mundo
No hay luces alrededor
Lleno de un espacio vacío
No sé dónde estoy
No sé cómo soy
Solo estoy llenando una cáscara vacía
Escondiéndome detrás de una máscara
Nadie sabe quién soy
Escondiendo todo

JUAN ELIZONDO es alumno de doceavo grado y actualmente asiste a la escuela preparatoria La Joya Early College. A Juan en su tiempo libre le gusta jugar juegos. Le gusta escribir sobre la vida.

Una amiga

Es alguien que siempre está allí para ti
En las buenas y en las malas
Una amiga es esa persona que siente por ti
Y no te abandona cuando las cosas se ponen difíciles
Es esa persona que te levanta cuando te tropiezas, no se burla de ti
Es esa persona que hace todo lo posible para sacarte una sonrisa
Cuando estás teniendo un mal día o nada más necesitas un levantamiento de ánimo.

BRISA ADAME-PEÑA es alumna de onceavo grado y actualmente asiste a la preparatoria La Joya Early College. Adame-Peña en su tiempo libre le gusta cantar y hacer postres. Le gusta escribir sobre sus experiencias románticas, sus amigos y las cosas hermosas que le pasan. Ha sido publicada en Poetry Cafe.

Poema 1

A los ancianos a menudo nunca se les toma en serio,
aunque son viejos,
son almas sabias.

Los jóvenes a menudo ignoran a las personas mayores,
pensando que están diciendo tonterías,
poco saben que han experimentado mucho más.

Las personas mayores a menudo son vistas como tristes debido a la edad,
sin embargo, son más felices de lo que piensas.
El hecho de que no puedan moverse tanto como los jóvenes
no significa que todavía no puedan encontrar una manera de divertirse.
Los domingos de bingo son tan divertidos como los viernes por la noche para
los jóvenes.

Las personas mayores a menudo nunca son tomadas en serio,
los jóvenes a menudo ignoran a las personas mayores,
las personas mayores a menudo son vistas como tristes debido a la edad,
pero las personas mayores son más felices de lo que puedas imaginar.

SUSANA LEAL es alumno de décimo grado y actualmente asiste a La Joya Early
College Escuela secundaria. A Susana en su tiempo libre le gusta ir de compras
y ver películas. Le gusta escribir sobre experiencias y desafíos de la vida real.

Qué pasará

Qué pasará cuando ya no escuche tus llamadas
Cuando la casa pierda su calor
Cuando ya no sea un "dulce hogar"
Qué pasará cuando el silencio se haga tan ruidoso que no lo soporte
Cuando los mire llorando por ti
Cómo las lágrimas caen de su rostro
Por alguien que ya no está ahí
¿Que pasará?

DULCE MATA es alumno de décimo grado y actualmente asiste a la preparatoria La Joya Early College. A Dulce en su tiempo libre le gusta leer y hacer ejercicio. Le gusta escribir sobre su vida personal.

Cuando muramos

Cuando muramos ojalá pudiéramos convertirnos en ser parte de el hermoso cielo
De parte de todo el hermoso cielo
Para que cuando llueva
Estar entre la lluvia
y podamos estar en todas partes
En todas las partes que no pudimos
estar cuando estuvimos vivos.

AMÉRICA QUINTERO es alumna de onceavo grado y actualmente asiste a la preparatoria La Joya Early College. A América en su tiempo libre le gusta jugar fútbol. Le gusta escribir sobre la naturaleza y la vida.

La mejor estudiante

Ella es la mejor estudiante
Con su tarea siempre es constante
Cuando ven sus calificaciones todos la envidian
Y con ella cuando saca un setenta no se fastidian
Pero la mejor estudiante sí
La mejor estudiante empieza a llorar
Y empieza a suspirar
Todos los que la han admirado
Miran como se ha expresado
La verdad es que
Ser la mejor estudiante es una carga para ella
Se queda despierta noche tras noche estudiando
Y se sigue diciendo
estoy cansada
Estresada
Frustrada
Desesperada
Ya no soporto más el tormento
Pero mientras siga siendo la mejor estudiante
No importa como me sienta

ANAYELI es estudiante de décimo grado y asiste a la preparatoria La Joya Early College. A Anayeli en su tiempo libre le gusta escuchar música. Le gusta escribir sobre cualquier cosa que le venga a la mente. Disfruta dibujando a sus personajes para que encajen en la historias que escribe.

Azul

El color que tiene la variación más bonita
El color que vemos en el cielo
El color del océano eterno
El color que está en estas paredes de mi espacio seguro
Mi color favorito
Azul

Alguna persona

Alguna persona que se llama Él
Él es la persona que espero ver
Él siempre está vagando por los pasillos de mi mente
Él es la inspiración de mi creatividad
Él es todo
Él no es real
Él es el producto de mi imaginación

Mía

Ella me hizo creer en el destino
El destino nos unió
Ella pone una sonrisa en mi cara con su cola meneando
Cuando me siento triste ella se pone triste conmigo
La amo a pesar de que ya no sea una cachorrita
Su nombre es Mía y ella es mía

CRYSTALYNN CHÁVEZ es alumna de décimo grado y actualmente asiste a la preparatoria La Joya Early College.Crystalyn Chávez en su tiempo libre le gusta dormir y leer. Le gusta escribir sobre sus gustos.

Nuestra Navidad

A mí me gusta el invierno
No sé por qué será
No sé si será por el frío
O por la Navidad
También me gusta el frío
Por ponerme unos guantes
Y una chamarra también

LEONARDO R. es alumno de onceavo grado y actualmente asiste a la escuela preparatoria La Joya Early College. A Leonardo en su tiempo libre le gusta ver películas. Le gusta escribir sobre deportes.

Indecisa

Con tantos caminos de vida, no hay uno correcto,
El camino puede parecer peligroso y frío
pero
no elegir
Es como estar de pie en una tormenta de nieve
La comodidad a solo dos pasos de distancia

Este día

Un día continuaremos nuestros nuevos caminos de vida
Un día mis pensamientos se llenarán sin ti en ellos
Un día el sol amanecerá sin ti a mi lado
Un día serás solo un recuerdo
Un día nos pasaremos como extraños
Un día voy a olvidar tus labios que me sonríen tan cálidamente
Un día esa risa tan rara que me encanta escuchar ya no la oiré yo
Pero
Este día espero que sigas siendo mi Valentín

Contigo

Ciega a ti
por mi ignorancia
mis muchas luchas

SARAH GARZA es alumna del décimo grado y actualmente asiste a La Joya Early College. A Sarah Graza en su tiempo libre gusta ver documentales. Le gusta escribir sobre lo que le ocurre y sobre su estado de ánimo.

Poema 1

Atrapada en mis sueños,
prisionera en mis recuerdos,
nunca te dejaré ir,
ni aunque estemos en desacuerdo.

Negaré todo lo malo de ti,
para mí eres la pequeña yo,
con solo recordarte,
me llevas a bellos recuerdos.

Grandes recuerdos de hermosas escenas,
una sonrisa muy bella,
que me hace extrañar los viejos tiempos.

ÁNGELA COLÓN es alumna de onceavo grado y actualmente asiste a La Joya Early College Escuela secundaria. A Ángela Colón en su tiempo libre le gusta leer. Le gusta escribir sobre sus recuerdos.

El árbol leal

Hay un árbol
Siéntate debajo del árbol y tendrás paz.
Paz y sombra del sol.

El árbol se destaca
Ondea en el viento
Se mueve cada vez que sopla una ráfaga de viento

Es otoño
Las hojas son rojas y naranjas.
Millones de hojas en el suelo del árbol.

Este árbol es alto
Los árboles alrededor de este árbol no se comparan con este
Este árbol es leal a la persona debajo de él.

Este árbol protege a su persona del sol.
Y es una sombra magnífica.

Este árbol es leal, leal a cualquiera debajo de él.
Protege a las personas del sol, con sus hojas
Incluso después de que sus hojas sean arrastradas por la ráfaga de viento.

The loyal tree

There is a tree
Sit under the tree and you'll get peace
Peace and shade from the sun.

The tree stands out
It waves around in the wind
It moves every time a gust of wind blows

It's Fall
Leaves are red, and orange
Millions of leaves on the ground from the tree

This tree is tall
Trees around this tree don't compare to this one
This tree is loyal to the person under it

This tree protects its person from the sun
And its shade, magnificent.

This tree is loyal, loyal to anyone under it
It protects people from the sun, with its leaves
Even after its leaves are blown by the gust of wind.
Pero
Este día espero que sigas siendo mi Valentín

Diego Treviño es alumno de grado 11 y actualmente asiste a la escuela preparatoria La Joya Early College. Diego Treviño, en su tiempo libre, le gusta jugar y cocinar. Le gusta escribir sobre cosas al azar que vienen a la mente.

i am

i am the very first
slice of bread
nobody wants to eat
i'm the seeds buried
in your bouncy weed
and that one
lightbulb that broke
and ruined your
string of lights
i'm the feeling you
get when you hear
an amber alert
i'm the old razor you
find lying around
when you've just got
home from another
day that was the
same as yesterday
and is going to be
the same as
tomorrow
i'm the restlessness
the nights before
first and last days

Luisa "Bella" Vidaurre is a high school student from McAllen, TX. First place winner of the 2016 Youth Creative Writing Contest from the McAllen Book Festival for her poem Moving On. Luisa likes to go to concerts and travel. She is proud of her Salvadoran-Mexican heritage.

IV.

VIPF CONTRIBUTORS/ COLABORADORES DE VIPF

Abubakar Auwal is a multilingual teen poet, playwright, essayist, movie actor, graphics designer, storyteller and also a spoken word artist born in Minna, Niger State, Nigeria. He is a member of The Poetic Collective (TPC VIII) and a founding-member of The Young Nigerlite Spoken word Artist (TYNSWA_1_).

Adrian Ernesto Cepeda is the author of *Flashes & Verses... Becoming Attraction*s from Unsolicited Press, *Between the Spine* from Picture Show Press, *Speaking con su Sombra* with Alegría Publishing, *La Belle Ajar & We Are the Ones Possessed* from CLASH Books and his 6th poetry collection *La Lengua Inside Me* will be published by FlowerSong Press in 2023.

Adrian lives with his wife in Los Angeles with their adorably spoiled cat Woody Gold.

AJRR, Adriana Rodríguez (1984) H. Matamoros, Tamaulipas; México. Ha participado en eventos de poesía local, virtuales y programas literarios. Colaborando en diversas antologías. Publicado narrativa en diferentes revistas digitales. Integrante del grupo Hacedores de fuego de la casa del Poeta Reino Unido, activista de paz IFLAC World México.

Mr. Alan Cherian Puthenpurayil (ACP) is a bilingual poet and critic from India who has notched up a significant place in the literary field. He has won numerous awards in state, national and international levels. He is currently the Official Member of WUP [World Union of Poets, Italy], HPAW [Hafrikan Prince Arts World, Ghana], the Indian representative of WNWU [World Nation Writers Union, Kazakhstan], the official member of ALLM [Academia Latinamericana Literatura Moderna, Mexico] and the official member of ICFHC[International Cultural Forum for Humanity and Creativity, Syria].

Aldo Cristian Méndez Castillo was born in Valles City, in San Luis Potosí, Mexico. Since he can remember he always loved to write, write dreams, memories and poetry, in english and spanish.

He is trying to be better and more creative in his poems, stories and short tales.

Alejandro Chang Hernández. Desde pequeño el autor se inclinó por la literatura. Participó en varios concursos, obteniendo premios. La pandemia permite escribir más y comienza a publicar: revistas Letras y Voces, Afrodita, Doble Voz, Iguales, La Ninfa Eco, El Creacionista, Trinando. Tiene publicado un libro de poesía titulado Palabras de un Poeta Aficionado.

Alejandro Zapata Espinosa (Colombia, 2002), estudiante de Licenciatura en Literatura y Lengua Castellana, escribe cuentos, poemas y columnas en *Al Poniente*. Es parte de la *Antología de poesía* (Trinando Editores, 2022). Mención de Honor en el 79º Concurso Internacional de Poesía y Narrativa «Camino de Palabras» (2023).

Alekhine Rebaza. Escritor nacido en Lima en 1970. En 2012 escribió la novela corta "La Luna Mochica". Se han publicado poemas suyos en la revista Trinando (Colombia-Méjico) y está preparándose una publicación, también de poemas de su autoría, en la editorial madrileña Lord Byron.

Aleksandra Lekić Vujisić (Podgorica, Montenegro) is a professor of English and an award-winning writer of prose and poetry. Aleksandra writes in her native language and English, and her poetry has been translated into Spanish, Italian, Polish, Chinese and other languages. She is a co-author of more than 50 anthologies, and an author of a poetry book "Bleeding in my letters" (Publishing house Poetikum, Serbia, 2022).

Allan Lake, originally from Saskatchewan, has lived in Vancouver, Cape Breton, Ibiza, Tasmania, W.Australia & Melbourne. Lake has won Lost Tower Publications (UK) Comp, Melbourne Spoken Word Poetry Festival & publication in New Philosopher. Latest poetry chapbook (Ginninderra Press) '*My Photos of Sicily*'. Literary journals in 16 countries have now published his poems; 70 were published in 2022.

Ana Saldaña (Mexico City, 1995) studied German literature at the National Autonomous University of Mexico (UNAM). She has participated in workshops with Mexican writers Elisa Díaz Castelo and Cecilia Magaña. Her work has appeared in anthologies and publications, including *Novísimas: Reunión de poetas mexicanas vol. II* (2021) and *Ágora. Revista del Centro de Estudios Internacionales del Colegio de México* (2018).

Andrés Mijangos Labastida, nació en la ciudad de Comitán de Domínguez, Chiapas. Estudió Filosofía en la Universidad Nacional Autónoma de México. Ha publicado cuento, poesía, y minificción, en diversas revistas digitales. Fue parte del V Diplomado Virtual de Creación Literaria de la Coordinación Nacional de Literatura. Actualmente forma parte del PECDA Chiapas, en la categoría de cuento.

Anita Howard (Cork, Ireland), is a writer, storyteller and actor living in Passage West, Co. Cork. Her work features in various publications, including HeadStuff, Poetica Review, the Sweetycat Press *Zooanthology*, the Querencia Press Autumn 22 Anthology and the December 2022 *Mslexia Moth*. She is on Twitter as @AnitaHowardSto1.

Antonio Ramírez Córdova. Puerto Rico (1941). Egresado de la Universidad de Barcelona (1968). Es poeta, dramaturgo, ensayista, narrador, crítico literario y catedrático universitario jubilado.

Premios: Editorial Mairena (1984), Pen Club (1985), Certamen Nacional de Poesía: JGB (2009), XI Festival Internacional de Poesía de PR: VRN (2019), II Certamen Nacional de Poesía: HSB (2022).

Ashlynn Delias is a student at Southwestern University. She self-published her first poetry book, *Beauty and Ashes*, in 2022. Aside from poetry, she enjoys writing lifestyle articles about wellness and relationships. She is currently a National Writer at Her Campus and is the AEIC at her school's paper, *The Megaphone*.

Baltazar Cordero Tamez, Ingeniero Químico de profesión
Fue presidente del Circulo literario Dr, Manuel F. Rodriguez Brayda y co-fundador del Ateneo Literario José Arrese .En 2001 ganó el Premio Estatal de Periodismo Manuel Buendía en Tamaulipas por Artículo de Fondo además de un tercer lugar en el certamen estatal de Crónica cultural.

Ha publicado en revistas digitales y su trabajo se incluye además, en varias antologías nacionales y extranjeras donde ha compartido sus cuentos y poemas en español con escritores de todo el mundo.

Bertha Galán Poeta boliviana. Escritora, poeta y profesora de Literatura. Nació en Bolivia. Desde la adolescencia tiene el gusto y la pasión por la escritura. Participó en el Concurso Internacional Club Literario "Versos desde el Pilcomayo" obteniendo el primer lugar en poesía. Participó en el Festival de Arte Sur Andino Arica Barroca, logrando el primer lugar en la categoría poesías. Tiene participación en antologías nacionales e internacionales (Bolivia, España, México, Argentina, Chile e Indonesia) Asimismo, su poesía ha sido publicada en diferentes revistas impresas y digitales. Tiene participación activa en Grupos Literarios Internacionales.

Binod Dawadi (Nepal) is the author of The Power of Words, is a master's degree holder in Major English. He has worked on more than 1000 anthologies published in various renowned magazines. His vision is to change society through knowledge, so he wants to provide enlightenment to the people through his writing skills.

Bruce McRae, a Canadian musician, is a multiple Pushcart nominee with poems published in hundreds of magazines such as Poetry, Rattle and the North American Review. The winner of the 2020 Libretto prize and author of four poetry collections and seven chapbooks, his poems have been performed and broadcast globally.

Candace Meredith earned her Bachelor of Science degree in English Creative Writing from Frostburg State University in 2008. Her works of poetry, photography and fiction have appeared In various small presses. She also earned her Master of Science degree in Integrated Marketing and Communications (IMC) from West Virginia University. She currently lives in the Shenandoah Valley of Virginia with her fiancé, two sons, daughter, eight cats and four dogs.

Carmen Calatayud is the author of *In the Company of Spirits* (Press 53), a runner up for the Academy of American Poets Walt Whitman Award. Her poetry and nonfiction appears in Beltway Poetry Quarterly, Manifest-Station, Verse Daily and several anthologies. She lives and writes in San Antonio, Texas.

Carmen Gray, Texas, USA
Carmen Gray is a Native Texan. She has appeared 3 times in different volumes of Road Kill: Texas Horror by Texas Writers. She also authored 2 short stories published by Caste Bridge Media.

She is an editor for Latino magazine and is currently working on a novel in progress.

Chepy Salinas Domínguez (Tiltepec, Jiquipilas, Chiapas, México)
Egresada de la Esc. Normal Superior de Chiapas. Maestra en pedagogía y Doctora en Ciencias de la educación. Ha participado en lecturas de poesía de su autoría en el Encuentro al sur de la palabra en San Cristóbal de las Casas, Museo del Café, Museo de la Marimba, en el centro cultural Jaime Sabines con el escritor Eraclio Zepeda en Evento de Círculo Editorial Azteca, XXIV Encuentro Internacional de Mujeres Poetas en el País de las Nubes. Lectura en la sala Boari de Bellas Artes, Cdmx. Encuentro Sureñas en Bacalar, Quintana Roo, En el Cervantino callejero en Guanajuato con CletaUnam, Encuentro

Ágora y selva en Palenque, Chiapas. Antologada en los poemarios colectivos Des- nudos entre la imagen y el verso, Destellos que arden, Palabras en Libertad, cántaro de voces, Cofre de Cedro editado por Círculo Azteca., Mujeres poetas por la paz XXIV, XXV, y XXVII., en la Revista Va de Nuez de Guadalajara, La aldaba en la arena de Colectivo entrópico., Brujas II y Mujeres en la palabra de ediciones Aquelarre., Revista Digital Piraña, Periódico El Machete. Poesía desde la coyuntura: Voces para caminar(CLETA-UNAM). Sureñas del Forcazs Coneculta, universo poético compilado por la poeta Socorro Trejo Sirvent. Libros de su autoría Cielo rojo, Galería de Soledades, Letanía de soles viejos. Promotora cultural de Maya Cartonera.

Chim Sher Ting
Sher Ting is a Singaporean-Chinese currently residing in Australia. She is a Pushcart and Best of The Net nominee with work published/ forthcoming in OSU The Journal, The Pinch, Salamander, and elsewhere. Her chapbook, *Bodies of Separation*, is forthcoming with Cathexis Northwest Press. She tweets at @sherttt and writes at sherting.carrd.co

Christopher T. Dabrowski is a Polish writer and screenwriter. His books have been published in Poland, the USA, Canada, Spain and Germany. His stories were published in many countries: USA, England, Australia, Canada, Poland, Russia, Germany, India, Slovakia, Czech Republic, Brasil, Spain, Argentina, Italy, Hungary, Sweden, Mexico, Albania, Nigeria, Botswana, Zimbabwe, Tanzania, Uganda, Kenya, Costa Rica, Peru, Vietnam, Turkey, Ukraine, Romania, Portugal, Tunisia, Bosnia & Herzegovina, Bangladesh & Slovenia.

Claudia Elisa Saquicela Novillo. Estudió en el Colegio Rosa de Jesús Cordero (Mejor egresada, medalla de oro). Habla inglés a nivel TOEFL. Obtuvo el diploma DELF B2 y el C1 en francés. Es psicóloga de la Universidad de Cuenca y abogada de la UTPL. Tiene una maestría en Educación y Desarrollo del pensamiento de la Universidad de Cuenca. Fue ganadora del 3er concurso a mejor proyecto de investigación de la Universidad de Cuenca DIUC. Tiene un postgrado en Comercio Exterior FEDEXPORT. Ha estudiado diseño gráfico y poesía en el Instituto de Artes de la Universidad de California CALARTS.

Dee Allen [Oakland, California U.S.A.--traditional land of the Ohlone Nation] African-Italian performance poet based in Oakland, California. Author of 7 books--Boneyard, Unwritten Law, Stormwater, Skeletal Black, Elohi Unitsi, Rusty Gallows and Plans--and 61 anthology appearances. Currently seeking a new publisher to transform his finished manuscript into a finished, printed 8th book.

Denise Melanie Du Lagrosa Is a poet, lyricist, songwriter, performing artists from the Philippine with Filipino Chinese heritage roots from Antipolo, Rizal, Bicol and Quezon, Philippine. She is known as Ms. Shakespeare in her alma mater for her writing & eloquent public speaking. She won 2nd Place for Ecosongwriters Festival. She is an active member of International Singer Songwriter Association. She has a page *PoetRx Pandemic Medic Poetry for a Pill where she shares her poetry and other writings during the time of pandemic.*

2023 VIPF FEATURED POET: Diosa Xochiquetzalcóatl, or Diosa X for short, is a multilingual and multidimensional Xicana, Indigenous, MeXicana poetiza. She has featured, presented, and performed nationally and internationally at open mics, literary events, poetry festivals, local libraries and slam competitions. She has been published in literary journals and magazines as well as several anthologies in both English and Spanish. Diosa X is the author of two poetry collections, with a third collection on the way: *A Church of My Own* (2021), *Hechizera: Sus Sultry Spells* (2022), and *West of the Santa Ana and a few Other Sacred Places* (2023).

Dorthy LaVern Spencer McCarthy has published ten books of short stories and poetry. She has won five hundred state awards for her poetry and thirty-four national awards. She is a life member of the Poetry Society of Texas. She resides in Blair Oklahoma.

Douglas Colston (Australia) has written throughout his life. In the distant past, he wrote a postgraduate thesis, political speeches and songs and lyrics for Ska bands. His nonfiction, fiction and poetry has been published in various journals and now – among other things – he is pursuing a PhD in Creative Writing.

Doug Croft's first full-length poetry collection, *Exposed Roots*, was published in early 2023. Croft lives in North Carolina from where he works, writes, spends time with his two adult children, and travels to see as many of his favorite rock 'n' roll bands as possible.

Dr. Olivier Pascalin Renowned international author of several books such as "Dancing Knowing Your Body", "Noel in Paraguay", "The Eternal Apprentice", Unicuentos", etc... Olivier Pascalin, alias El Doc is a Doctor of Medicine founder of Medics without borders (MSF) and recognized throughout the world for his work in natural, energetic and integrative health.

E. Martin Pedersen, originally from San Francisco, has lived for over forty years in eastern Sicily, where he taught English at the local university. He has published two collections of haiku, *Bitter Pills* and *Smart Pills,* and a chapbook, *Exile's Choice*, from Kelsay Books.
(E. Martin Pedersen, Italy)

Eduardo Omar Honey Escandón. (México, 1969) Ing. en sistemas. Participante desde los 90s en talleres literarios bajo la guía de diversos escritores. Publica constantemente en plaquettes, revistas físicas, virtuales e internet. Textos suyos fueron primero, segundo, tercer lugar o finalistas. Ha sido seleccionado para participar en diversas antologías.

Edward Lee (Ireland) Edward Lee's poetry, short stories, non-fiction and photography have been published in magazines in Ireland, England and America, including The Stinging Fly, Skylight 47, Acumen, The Blue Nib and Poetry Wales. His play 'Wall' received a rehearsed reading as part of Druid Theatre's Druid Debuts 2020.

He also makes musical noise under the names Ayahuasca Collective, Orson Carroll, Lego Figures Fighting, and Pale Blond Boy.

Elisa A. Garza (Texas, USA) has published two chapbooks, *Entre la Claridad* (Mouthfeel Press, second edition 2023) and *Familia* (The Portlandia Group). Individual poems currently appear in *The Bayou Review, Amarillo Bay,* and *Texas Poetry Assignment.* She has taught in public schools, universities, and community programs and works as a freelance editor.

Enedina Irene is a San Antonio-raised poet, prose writer, romance novelist, and spoken word performer. Her works have been featured in the Mujer –Centric Zine, St. Sucia, and on the Texas Public Radio program, Worth Repeating.

Enrique Manuel Infante Ángeles (23 de abril de 1972)
Músico, escritor y compositor peruano radicado en la ciudad de Houston. Estudió solfeo y teoría musical y, posteriormente, Administración de Empresas y Taekwondo.

En Lima, trabajó con las agrupaciones teatrales "Abeja" y "Dantemus", y con las bandas "Los Mojarras", "Pukakuntur" y "Visos de Burdeos". En Columbus, Ohio, fundó "Dejavu Latin Fusion Rhythms" y la "Sociedad de escritores de Columbus". Cursó múltiples talleres de poesía, narrativa y escritura creativa.

Como autor, ha participado en diversos festivales presenciales y virtuales, entre las que se destaca, la segunda edición de la "Feria internacional del libro de Nueva York". Enrique Infante es miembro activo de ASCAP (Asociación Americana de Autores, Compositores y Editores), LARAS (Academia Latina de Artes y Ciencias de la Grabación) y NARAS (Academia Americana de Artes y Ciencias de la Grabación).

Érika Elisa Garza is originally the magic town of Cd. Mier, Tamaulipas, Mexico. Garza has published in numerous anthologies including *Dreaming: A Tribute To Selena Quintanilla-Pérez*, *Resplandores Poéticos: primera antología de poetas colombianos y latinoamericanos* and *Boundless* (2018-2022). She is the author of the poetic collection *Con alas de Mariposa*.

Estrella Gracia González, 13. Noviembre. 1979, H. Matamoros, Tamaulipas. Lic. En ciencias de la comunicación. Participa en antologías como: No basta con cerrar los ojos en la sombra(Winged,2022); Homenaje a escritoras y escritores Contemporáneos de Tamaulipas; La fantasía en todas sus formas y Súbita convergencia (Alja,2022).

Ha publicado en revistas digitales nacionales e internacionales.

Felix Cardoso. Nació en el corazón de la Cultura Matlazinca, Calixtlahuaca. Toluca, México. Ha publicado: *"Éxodo al Génesis"* 2020 Edición Bilingüe (Inglés-Español) Editorial Dark Light, *"Disfrutando mis pecados"* 2020, "*Sabor a piel*", 2012; "*Trazos en la piel*", 2010; "*Navegar en la piel*", 2009. Poesía amorosa-sensual-erótica. Además las plaquette´s *"La hojarasca vuelve a nacer"*, y *"Sin el Aroma de tu rezo"*, 2005. Aparece en más de cuarenta antologías tanto de narrativa como de poesía. Ha participado en encuentros Nacionales e Internacionales.

G. Libedinsky is a Mexican poet who has published 2 books in Mexico and has been part of various anthologies and poetry festivals around the world (Argentina, Spain, Costa Rica, Mexico, Morocco, France, etc.). His style is melancholic and depressing but still contains a bit of hope.

Nacido en Barranquilla, Colombia: **Santiago Domínguez. Refugiado** siempre en la música y la literatura, desea aprovechar la oportunidad de publicar con ustedes. «Envío Juvenil».

Gabriel González Núñez es profesor de La Universidad de Texas en el Valle del Río Grande. Ha publicado diez libros para niños (Penguin Random House Uruguay 2019, 2020, 2021, 2022), el poemario Ese golpe de luz (FlowerSong Press 2020) y el plaquette digital bilingüe El ciclo / The Cycle (Center for Latter-day Saint Arts 2020). También ha publicado poemas en revistas y antologías. Además es autor de la colección de cuentos Rumbos (Jade Publishing 2021) y tradujo el poemario Vaho / Mist del poeta salvadoreño Javier Fuentes Vargas. González Núñez es oriundo de Montevideo, Uruguay.

Gabriella Gutiérrez y Muhs has been a poet since childhood. She has five collections of poetry: *The Plastic Book, A Most Improbable Life, The Runaway Poems, Frontera Dogs*, and recently published *¿How Many Indians Can We Be? ¿Cuántos Indios podemos ser?* with Flowersong Press, and other collections forthcoming. She has published her work in various journals, among them: *The Yellow Medicine Review, The Red Wheelbarrow, The MALCS Journal, Ventana Abierta, Puentes, Camino Real.* She has edited two major anthologies of Chicanx/Latinx poetry: *In Xochitl, in cuícatl,* (Polibea Press, Madrid) and *Indomitable: Indomable*s, with San Diego State University Press, 2023.

Gerald Jatzek is a poet, musician, and mail artist from Vienna, Austria, who writes in German and English. He has published books and songs for children and adults. His poems have appeared in anthologies and magazines in Europe, India and the USA.

Gerry Rodriguez is a poet and playwright from Mission, TX. She holds an MFA in Creative Writing from University of Texas Rio Grande Valley. Her work has appeared in *Stonecrop Magazine, decomp journal, Open Minds Quarterly*, and others.

G.G. (Giana Gallardo) Hesterberg was born and raised in Brownsville, Texas. She published her first book, *Stories by the Seashore,* in March of 2019. Her second book, *Music, Music, You Can Too!*, a nonfiction children's book, was released in July 2020.

Guna Moran is an internationally acclaimed assamese poet and book reviewer from Assam,India.His poems are published in more than 200 hundred international magazines,journals and have been translated into 30 languages around the world.He has five poetry books to his credit.Gloves in Assam, India.

Gustavo Barahona-López is a writer and educator from Richmond, California.

His chapbook, "Loss and Other Rivers That Devour", was published by Nomadic Press. Barahona-López's full-length collection, "Foundation" is forthcoming from FlowerSong Press. A VONA alum, Barahona-López's work can be found in Honey Lit. among other publications.

Irlyan del Carmen Hernández Sosa de Bacalar, Quintana Roo, imparte talleres de poesía. Dirige el Club de Lectura "Lectores en Acción" Ganó tercer lugar en el IV Concurso Nacional de Poesía Joven Amapola Fenochio 2020 del Estado de Puebla, con la antología "Amor a una sombra y otros poemas" Esta participación se trata de un envío juvenil.

Iván Medina tiene tres libros publicados: *En cualquier lugar fuera de este mundo* (CONACULTA, 2012), *Más frío que la muerte* (UAM, 2017*)* y *Lugares ajenos (*BUAP, 2020). Becario del Programa de Residencias Artísticas FONCA-CONACYT. Es doctorando en Arte y Literatura en la Universidad de Guanajuato.

Jackie Kabir, **Dhaka Bangladesh** is a writer and a translator. Her collection of short stories Silent Noise was published by Pathak Samabesh in 2016. The titular story 'Silent Noise' is being taught in BA English course (South-Asian literature in English) in colleges under Manomanium Sundaram University, Tirunelveli. Tamil Nadu.

Jasmin Garcia is an RGV-based poet. Her works can be found published in La Bloga (2017), VIPF Boundless Anthology (2018), and I SING: THE BODY (2021). Garcia has read at venues across the Rio Grande Valley, her debut collection of poetry *Paper Crane* (Esperanza Publishing) is due out in 2023. You can follow her on her Instagram, @thecafepoet.

2023 VIPF FEATURED POET: Javier Villarreal, a Professor Emeritus of Spanish, holds a BA and MA in Spanish from Pan American University, Edinburg (UTRGV), and a Ph.D. in Hispanic Linguistics from the University of Texas at Austin. His works have appeared in numerous academic and literary journals and anthologies. His first poetry collection Entre Lluvia, canto y flor was published in 2008, and Perfiles del silencio in 2021. He edited La voz de amor of Servando Cárdenas in 2016. He is a member of the People's Poetry Festival. Javier retired from Texas A&M University-Corpus Christi in 2015. He resides in Corpus Christi with his family, where he writes, practices photography, and promotes cultural events in South Texas.

Jean Hackett lives and writes in San Antonio and the Texas Hill Country in the USA. Her chapbook *Masked/Unmuted* was published in March 2022.

jo reyes-boitel is a poet and playwright, queer mixed Latinx, amateur hand percussionist, and parent now working on their MFA in Creative Writing at the University of Texas – Rio Grande Valley, where they also serve as an undergraduate instructor. Their publications include *Michael + Josephine*, a novel in verse (FlowerSong Press, 2019) and the chapbook *mouth* (Neon Hemlock, 2021) as well as *playing with fire*, forthcoming from Next Page Press in November 2023. "she wears bells", their hybrid opera, was chosen as a finalist for Guerilla Opera's 2022 annual virtual festival. For more information about jo and their work visit joreyesboitel.com.

Joann González is a 22 year old artist, based in Texas, USA. For her, writing has always been one of the most sincere ways of getting to know oneself and the world around them. Present day, Joanncombines her filmmaking and love for poetry to express her own unique version of storytelling.

John Chinaka Onyeche is an author, poet, and teacher of History and African History. He is the author of "25 Atonements", A husband, father and poet from Nigeria. John composes his work from the city of Port Harcourt Rivers State, Nigeria. He is currently a student of History and Diplomatic Studies at Ignatius Ajuru University of Education Port Harcourt Rivers State. When John is not writing, he loves reading.

John C. Mannone, Kentucky, USA, awarded a Jean Ritchie Fellowship (2017), has poems in *Windhover*, *North Dakota Quarterly*, *Poetry South*, *Baltimore Review*, and others. His forthcoming collections (2023) are *Sacred Flute* (Iris Press) and *Song of the Mountains* (Middle Creek Publishing). He's a physics professor at Alice Lloyd College.

Joselin Mejía Garcia, Mexico. Her poems have been published in Mexico and Chile by the UNAM, Bitácora de vuelos ediciones, Capicúa Editorial and La Gata Ediciones. Her poetry has also appeared in the USA in the 2021 and 2022 editions of The Anthology of the Rio Grande Valley International Poetry Festival.

José Rodolfo Espinosa Silva. H. Matamoros, Tamaulipas, México (1990). Escritor y profesor mexicano. Primer lugar en el IX Concurso de Cuento infantil CEAC 2022. Becario del PECDA Tamaulipas en la categoría de Jóvenes

Creadores por novela. Finalista en el Primer Concurso Nacional de Poesía Emergente Antonio Alatorre. Finalista en el Premio Ariadna de Poesía 2021.

José Luis Moreno, no es un poeta, es un aficionado a la poesía clásica de arte mayor y menor. Es de Reynosa Tamaulipas. Cuenta con un libro publicado 'La Poesía pide la palabra' y escribe para la revista Ecos Literarios, José Luis Calderón Vela de León Guanajuato.

Juan Manuel Perez is a Mexican-American of Indigenous descent and the author of multiple books of poetry. Juan currently resides in Corpus Christi, Texas. To learn more about him, visit his official website at: www.juanmperez.com

Julia-Paz, South Texas, USA, has been writing her whole life, from creative writing, research, journalism, and her favorite poetry. She has taken the time to really work on what she calls "conversations" between her pen and paper. Julia-Paz spends her time writing on healing, grief, and heartbreak themes.

Kim Malinowski (USA) earned her B.A. from West Virginia University and her M.F.A. from American University. Afterwards, medication caused aphasia. She relearned to read and write but still struggles. She has been nominated for the Pushcart Prize, Best of Net, and the Rhysling Award. She is fighting for the Nobel Prize.

Laura Peña was born and raised in Houston, Texas. She holds a BA in English Literature and an MA in Education. Currently she is a primary bilingual teacher in Houston. She has been published in *Diversity* from the Austin International Poetry Festival; Houston Poetry Fest anthology; *Boundless* from the Valley International Poetry Festival; Texas Poetry Calendar; hotpoet, and various other anthologies both in print and on-line. She was the featured poet at the April 2018 Valley International Poetry Festival in McAllen, Tx. Laura received the Lucille Johnson Clark Memorial Award at the 2018 Houston Poetry Fest that is awarded annually to the top juried poet who is also a K-12 classroom teacher. Laura has been a featured poet at Inprint's First Friday and Public Poetry. She has performed as part of Invisible Lines most recently for "Welcome to the American Freakshow" and "Each New Journey; Actual Slices of the Fabulous Billie Duncan".

Luisa Govela lives in Tampico, Mexico. She has a BA in both English and Spanish Language and Literature from the UNAM (National Autonomous

University of Mexico) She writes poetry, narrative, essays, and is also a translator. She has published seven books, among which are: :A Time for Words, Peninsula of the Wind; The Beloved Enemy, Mirrors of Time. Her poems, essays, and stories have been published in anthologies and magazines in Mexico, the United States and Italy. She is a frequent invited writer in the San Miguel de Allende Poetry Week and in Letras en la Frontera in San Antonio, Tex. She has taken graduate courses in the University of Lancaster in Lancashire, U.K. and in the University of Saint Mark and Saint John in Devon, U.K. and has an MBA in Education from Lesley College, Cambridge, Mass. USA. Her favorite activities now are reading, writing and being a grandmother.

Marcella Prokop is a Colombian writer who lives and teaches in the Midwest. Her work has appeared in print or online in The Brooklyn Review, Ploughshares, The Christian Science Monitor, The Fourth River Online and PANK, among others.

Margaret Cantu-Sanchez, Texas, USA
Margaret Cantú-Sánchez is Visiting Assistant Professor of English at St. Mary's University. Her poetry has been featured in the *Texas Poetry Calendar 2021* and *2023, The San Antonio Review, and Dissident Voices*. Margaret's writing focuses on her summer experiences growing up with her maternal grandparents in the Rio Grande Valley.

2023 VIPF FEATURED POET: Mark Esperanza is an Edcouch-Elsa writer and currently teaches in the US-Mexico borderland city of McAllen, TX. He has been published in numerous anthologies such as Lamar Press' Writing Texas and Boundless 2022: the official anthology of the Rio Grande Valley International Poetry Festival. Esperanza will be presenting on his published short story "La Llorona de Mile 17" at the 2023 AWP Conference panel: "Weeping Women: La Llorona's Presence in Modern Latinx and Chicanx Lore."

Mark Fleisher, New Mexico, USA
Mark Fleisher has published five books of poetry -- with some prose and photography added -- and contributed to a fifth. His work has appeared in online and print anthologies in the United States, Canada, the United Kingdom, Kenya, Nigeria and India. He holds a journalism degree from Ohio University.

Megha Sood is an Award-winning Asian American Poet, Editor, and Literary Activist from New Jersey. She is a Literary Partner with "*Life in Quarantine*", at Stanford University. Author of Full Length ("My Body Lives Like a Threat", FlowerSongPress,2022). She blogs at https://meghasworldsite.wordpress.com/ and tweets at @meghasood16.

Michael Gerleman has been a teacher in Harlingen for 35 years. He loves the Valley's vibrant cultural scene and appreciates those who make opportunities for local poets.

Michael Owens, Texas, USA
From Galveston Texas, Michael Owens is a botanist from Cypress Texas. Michael's work has been published in; Metonym Literary Journal at Jessup University, Red River Review, Houston Chronicle. His work has been in juried anthologies including Texas Poetry Calendar, Houston Poetry Fest, Texas Poetry Society, Austin International Poetry Society.

Mike Owsley (He/They) is a Missouri, USA based author and activist who can be best found on twitter @BigMikeOwsley. His short stories have previously appeared in The Castle of Horror Anthology. His poetry has previously appeared in Unstamatic, Palest Blue, and Poetry-as-Promised.

Miriam Romero, originaria del sur de Texas, es Profesora Asistente en la Universidad de Norwich. Su pasión por las letras la ha inspirado a buscar en la poesía una forma de expresión que va más allá del aula.

Mohammed U. Yusuf is a young writer and editor from North-Central, Nigeria. His works have recently appeared—or are forthcoming—in Frontier Poetry, RoseyRavelston Books, Lunaris Review, The Lumiere Review, Olongo Africa Journal, KonyaShamsrumi, among others. He is a Staff Reader at Chestnut Review and tweets @Unyomo.

Nancy Jo Allen lives in Columbia, Missouri, U.S.A.. Her first poetry collection, *Wrinkles in Time and in Love*, is available through Kelsay Books and Amazon. Her second collection will be published fall, 2023, through Kelsay Books and available also through Amazon.

Nelson Roque Pereira. Poeta, pertenece al Taller literario Olga Alonso, a las organizaciones POETAP en España y a ELILUC en Estados Unidos. Premiado en concursos, parte de su obra ha sido publicada en revistas, periódicos, plaquettes, boletines literarios, antologías internacionales y su poemario "Por los cauces de la noche", España, 2020.

Renowned international author of several books such as "Dancing Knowing Your Body", "Noel in Paraguay", "The Eternal Apprentice", Unicuentos", etc... **Olivier Pascalin**; alias El Doc is a Doctor of Medicine founder of Medics without borders (MSF) and recognized throughout the world for his work in natural, energetic and integrative health.

Paula Andrea Córdova García, México.
Andrea is a poet, writer, and student based in Mexico City. She earned a BA in Italian Literature from Universidad Nacional Autónoma de México and is currently studying Marketing. She co-founded the Red Universitaria de Mujeres Escritoras. Her work has been published in online media. The poem presented here was translated by Sandra Dolores Gomez Amador.

Peace Nkeiruka Maduako is a Nigerian writer often inspired by paintings and art that tell stories. She has works published on Calla Press, Kalahari Review, SpillWords Press, Brigitte Poirson Chapbook, ClayJar Review and more. She started writing as a girl but got her first online publication in September 2020. On Facebook she's "Peace Nkeiruka" https//www.facebook.com/peace.nkeiruka.56

PW Covington, New Mexico, USA
PW Covington is a former VIPF Featured Poet, writing in the Beat tradition of the North American highway. A multiple Pushcart and Best of the Net nominee, Covington presents his work for audiences across the nation. Keep up with him at www.PWCovington.com.

Ramiro Hernández Restrepo (Colombia, 1958) es profesional en Derecho y Ciencias Políticas, residente y domiciliado en Medellín, hijo de Raquel y Emilio. Atrapado por la poesía desde que vio una flor volando, y destrozado cuando un maestro le dijo que era una mariposa.

Rodrigo Miguel Quintero. Poeta y narrador argentino. Finalista de "Mundo literario 2004", 1° premio municipal de novela, finalista del concurso cuento breve "Las sombras del amor y la muerte 2021" (España). Colabora con: plataforma Medium, Herederos del Kaos, El Creacionista (México). Seguí su podcast: "Un día en la farmacia" y su blog: *https://relatosquevan.blogspot.com/*

Rolando Reyes López. (Pedro Betancourt. Matanzas. 1969). Reside desde el año 1971 en el municipio de Jovellanos. Matanzas. Cuba Graduado de Bachiller. Actualmente es jubilado por Baja Visión. Numerosos relatos breves y poemas suyos han sido publicados en 20 Antologías y 67 Revistas digitales de varios países de Europa y Latinoamérica.

Rolando Serna, La Villa Texas, United states
Started writing while in Federal Prison, attended UTPA and had a short story published while attending UTPA. Vice President of the Sigma tau Delta English Honor Society and published in Harper.

Roswel Borges Castellanos. Poemas suyos han aparecido publicados en "Viajando al Sur", Antología de Poetas Cubanos, Reina del Mar Editores, Cienfuegos (2006); en "Brotes", Boletín Cultural de la UNEAC de Villa Clara, (2007); en "Videncia", Revista Cultural de Ciego De Ávila, (2012); en "El Caimán Barbudo", Edición mayo-junio, (2014) y en Antología resultante del XXX Premio Mundial de Poesía Nósside 2014.

Roxana Arroyo (Mexico) is a graduate in English Literature and Language from Universidad Nacional Autónoma de México. In 2022 she was one of the selected participants for The Residency for Young Poets at Festival Internacional de Poesía de Rosario. Her Spanish-written poetry has been published in multiple online magazines.

Rubén Gerardo Santos Lezcano, La Habana, Cuba. En los tres últimos años ha dado a conocer su obra en diversas revistas. Trabajos suyos han aparecido publicado en varias antologías ("Crepusculares" de Editorial OXYMORON, "Como hermanos", Ediciones AFRODITA y "Desamor", Consejo Editorial Cordobés) Su poemario "Ciudad Dormida" apareció parcialmente en una antología especial de la revista TRINANDO.

Sandra Dolores Gómez Amador is a Mexican poet, interpreter, and translator. She earned a BA in English Literature from Universidad Nacional Autónoma de México in 2022. Her work has been published in both online and print media. She is an advocate for people convicted of a crime and individuals in immigration detention. ig: @sandradoloresam

Nacido en Barranquilla, Colombia: **Santiago Domínguez. Refugiado** siempre en la música y la literatura, desea aprovechar la oportunidad de publicar con ustedes. «Envío Juvenil».

Shannon Hardwick (USA) has work that has appeared, or is forthcoming, in Gulf Coast Journal, Salamander, South Dakota Review, The Texas Observer, Four Way Review, The Missouri Review, Sixth Finch, and Passages North, among others. A graduate of Sarah Lawrence College's MFA program, Hardwick serves as the Editor-in-Chief for The Boiler.

Sharanya B, India (Kerala State)
Sharanya lives in Trivandrum, Kerala and studies English literature. Her poems have appeared in several magazines and media such as LiveWire, The Madras Courier, Anthology by Poetry Society of India, Borderless Journal, Literary Vibes and so on. She won the fifth place in the Rabindranath Tagore International Poetry Competition 2022. Her poetry is forthcoming in The Unfolded Anthology (USA), and Indian Literature by Sahitya Akademi.

Shaswata Gangopadhyay -INDIA
One of the Prominent faces of Contemporary Indian Poetry
Shaswata has participated in different International poetry festivals in Europe and Both North and Latin America. His book of Poems : Inhabitant of Pluto Planet (2001), Offspring of Monster (2009), Holes of Red Crabs(2015), Rhododendron Cafe (2021),Selected Love Poems (2021), Altamira (2022) and In the City of Myth and Mushroom(2023).

Spartakos Anagnostaras was born in Athens in Greece. His poetry has appeared in North Dakota Quarterly, the Crank and Boundless 2022: the anthology of the Rio Grande Valley International Poetry Festival.

Stephen Douglas Wright is an author, educator, poet, and playwright, based in Michigan and Taiwan. His poems have been published in Boundless 2021 and Boundless 2022, and in other publications. His plays have been produced throughout the US and Taiwan. You can learn more about his work at stephendouglaswright.com.

Tabassum Tahmina Shagufta Hussein from Dhaka Bangladesh is International Fellow 2020 IHRAF. Poetry prize Award winner Korean Expatriate Literature 2021. She is the Translator, ITHACA Foundation Spain. Her poems have appeared in several literary magazines. She is a guest contributor to Different Truths India. She also contributes to Our Time and The Good Morning print newspaper Bangladesh.

Tania Jasso Blancas, Escritora, poeta y editora. Textos suyos aparecen en revistas y periódicos nacionales y extranjeros, así como en medios digitales. Ha colaborado en antologías y compilaciones publicadas en varios países. Es autora de los libros de poesía, Acusando al silencio, Merodeos y Poética y brevedad del hipopótamo, entre otros.

Terry Allen, Columbia, Missouri, is an emeritus professor of Theatre Arts at the University of Wisconsin-Eau Claire, where he taught acting, directing and playwriting. He is the author of the chapbook *Monsters in the Rain* and three full-length poetry collections: *Art Work, Waiting on the Last Train,* and *Rubber Time.*

2023 VIPF FEATURED POET: Thomas Ray Garcia is from Pharr, Texas, USA. At Princeton University, he received the Ward Mathis Short Story Prize for his U.S.-Mexico borderlands fiction. He is the author of the short story volume, The River Runs, and the co-author of El Curso de la Raza: The Education of Aurelio Manuel Montemayor.

TREV WAINWRIGHT, Although he has not been to the RGVIPF since 2019 Trev has featured in every Boundless since 2012, mostly poems about his travels.

UCHECHUKWU ONYEDIKAM (aka Mystic Poet) is a Nigerian creative artist from Lagos, Nigeria.

Víctor Hugo Orduña Silguero; originario de H. Matamoros Tamaulipas es Licenciado en Ciencias de la Comunicación con Maestría en Metodología de la Enseñanza; cantautor, fotógrafo, artista visual y poeta. Ha participado en diversas antologías de narrativa breve: "Brevedad urbana", "Dioses cortos y otros cuentos" y "Criaturas supersticiosas"; en antologías de poesías: "Confusión de cuerpos", "Ciudad de las palabras" y "Los días con otro nombre", todas publicadas por ALJA Ediciones. Formó parte de los Narradores Orales Escénicos de Tamaulipas. Ha sido invitado en diferentes ocasiones al Encuentro Binacional Letras en el Estuario. Ha ganado premios de poesía en el género de ciencia ficción y compuesto temas musicales para instituciones gubernamentales. Ganó el 1er. Lugar Estatal del Poetry Slam Tamaulipas 2019 en la FILIJ. Es catedrático de diferentes universidades, servidor público y autor del libro: Levitaciones "Cuentos muy breves para despertar".

2022 City of McAllen Poet Laureate and Author, **Victoria Lopez** -- Victoria writes Poetry on Demand, a performative demonstration of spontaneous writing. She is also the Founder of the Unfolded: Poetry Project, a community workshop series which promotes the reinforcement of individual and written voice.

Vito del Valle is a middle-aged punk rock/metal musician out of Donna, Texas. Vito writes songs and poems for his cats and whoever else is willing to listen.

Violeta Garza (Texas, USA) is a Latinx poet and performer. Her poems have been selected for Acentos Review, Voices de la Luna, and elsewhere. She has performed original poems and stories for Texas Public Radio and The Alamo Chapter for Human Rights. You can peruse her work at violetagarza.com.

Walter Alexis Velásquez Mendoza (Lima, Perú), Periodista, escritor y narrador. Ganador del premio literario COVID.19: Memorias de confinamiento y mención honrosa en el concurso de microrrelatos de la fundación Letra Viva.

Wendy B. Lara. Artista multifacética, reconocida por su desempeño actoral en teatro y televisión; como actriz, escritora y directora. Diseñadora y creadora de vestuarios.

Escritora de monólogos, libretos y poemas, incluidos en diferentes medios electrónicos y libros físicos. Su desempeño artístico tiene fundamento en el empoderamiento de la mujer y la fusión de las diferentes ramas artísticas.

William David, he lives in Edinburg Texas and holds two bachelor degrees from UTRGV. He has work appearing in last year's Boundless as well appearing in several other literary journals. He works in healthcare and as a tutor. He is currently working on putting together his first full length poetry manuscript.

Yelitza Tibisai Saenz is a writer from Roma, Tx. She has earned her Bachelor's Degree in English with a concentration in Creative Writing, along with a minor in Mexican American Studies. Saenz has performed her poetry at the Untamed Tongues: Poets Sin Fronteras Poetry Festival and at MXLAN 2022 Festival.

Born in "Brick City" Newark, NJ **Yari "Porta Rock" Pares** is an educator, writer, poet and activist using his craft to transmit lessons and messages of identity and social protest to the masses. He has a book titled, "From In Between the Bricks I Rise: Reflections from a Porta Rock."

Yonnier Torres Rodríguez (La Habana, 1981). Sociólogo, poeta y narrador. Entre sus últimos títulos publicados se encuentran los libros de cuentos "Puntos de luz" (Áncoras, 2015), "Quinientas formas de morir" (Reina del Mar, 2016), las novelas "Cerrar los puños" (Editorial Gente Nueva, 2015), "Azul pálido" (Ediciones La Luz, 2016) y el poemario "Dios no me tiene en cuenta" (Editora Abril, 2018). Cuentos y poemas suyos aparecen publicados en revistas, antologías y selecciones de España, Colombia, Argentina, Bolivia, Alemania. México y Cuba.

V.

EDITORS BIOS:

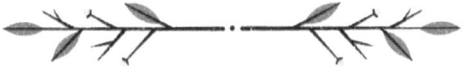

Linda Romero is from Harlingen, Texas, and has been published in the VIPF Boundless anthologies, Along the River 2: More Voices from the Rio Grande (VAO Publishing), Twenty: In Memoriam (El Zarape Press), and La Bloga. She was nominated for a Pushcart Prize in 2018 for her poem, "In the Passenger Seat" by El Zarape Press which appeared in Boundless 2017. She is a Certified Academic Language Therapist and has a private practice providing dyslexia therapy.

Eduardo Villarreal de los Reyes.
Su obra se incluye en "Poetas de Ayer y Hoy en Tamaulipas" (1983). En 1983 obtuvo el primer lugar en Cuento y en Poesía de la Facultad de Ciencias de la Comunicación (UANL). En 1985 es candidato al Premio Nacional de la Juventud CREA por el estado de Nuevo León en el renglón de Creación Literaria. En 1996 el Festival Internacional de Otoño le otorgó el Reconocimiento a las Expresiones del Arte. 2016 al presente, es Director Fundador del foro cultural binacional Poesía en Atril. Tiene publicados tres libros de poesíaAhora Pregunto Yo (2019), A Veces La Poesía (2020) y Todo De Nuevo (2020). En 2019 recibió un reconocimiento de la Academia de Literatura y Poesía de la SOGEM (Estado de México). En diciembre de 2022, la Secundaria Técnica número 4 "Gral. Lázaro Cárdenas", nombró a su biblioteca con el nombre Eduardo Villarreal de los Reyes.

Edward Vidaurre is an award-winning poet and author of eight collections of poetry. He is the 2018-2019 City of McAllen, Texas Poet Laureate, 2022 inductee to the Texas Institute of Letters, and publisher of FlowerSong Press. His writings have appeared in The New York Times Magazine, The Texas Observer, Los Angeles Review of Books, as well as other journals and anthologies. His new collection By Throat, By Miracle: New & Selected Poems will be out in 2023. Vidaurre resides in McAllen, Texas with his wife and daughter.

For details, visit our website at valleypoetryfest.org

www.ingramcontent.com/pod-product-compliance
Lightning Source LLC
Chambersburg PA
CBHW031508120626
46545CB00005B/1786